Leading with Light

A collection of thoughts from prominent light leaders

A CENTER OF INFLUENCE COMMUNITY ANTHOLOGY

Edited by Lil Barcaski and Linda Hinkle

Published by: Center of Influence Publishing
https://centerofinfluencecommunity.com/

Cover Design: Kristina Conatser

ISBN Print: 978-1-959608-47-9
ISBN eBook: 978-1-959608-46-2

Contents

Clare Williamson

Clare Williamson, the 'Millionaire Sha'Woman', is a Wayshower & Lightleader for the Visionaries who are ready to take their business to a 7-figure empire, the 'Awakened Way'. Clare integrates Breathwork, Shamanics and Somatics to clear, strategic steps for more income, impact and brand influence. Clare is a Motivational Speaker and Best-Selling Author. She gifts life-altering insight and profound healing to the Light Leader who is ready to go deeper and UNLEASH their Inner Millionaire! Clare's 'Awakened Wealth Blueprint' is accessible at various levels from her free Awakened Wealth app and Community through to her UNLEASHED Awakened Wealth 1:1, Mastermind and transformational retreats.

How Shamanism Will Save the World

By Clare Williamson

"Clare… Good luck with your shamanism, traditionally it takes 14 years to be a practicing shaman undergone with a full 1:1 apprenticeship. I sincerely hope that you use shamanism for the benefit of people for their wellbeing and as it traditionally happens, by donation. This whole millionaire stuff feeds into our egos which contributes to the pyramid system I am not wanting to belong to. For this reason, I dislike the whole coaching wealth and hell-ness industry that is just capitalism repackaged. Bob Marley's last words: 'Money doesn't buy you life.' People say that once you become a millionaire think of how many people's lives you can change, yet it seems like this never really happens. The rich continue to get richer and the poor are currently poorer than they have ever been. Just because the needs have switched doesn't mean to say that industry is not still industry. As the animistic saying goes, if your method doesn't grow corn, I am not interested."

In October 2022, I felt my rebirth. I heard the call from lifetimes ago to step onto the Shaman's path. I received this message privately from an ex-client as I started to "step out" with my new brand, "The Millionaire Sha'Woman." These words came to me deep in meditation, as I had been surrounded by spirit animals who willed me to hear their words… "It's time for you to make good on your promise, Clare."

I felt how the impact I had pledged to make, from childhood, had been squashed by my fears. I felt ready to face the rites of passage that would wake my lion's heart fully, so that fear would never block me from my Divine Will again. I saw how I am here to be the light in other people's darkness with my story and my soul talents. And I said yes to a whole new journey; a Soul Pilgrimage.

I knew I was going to trigger some criticism from pairing the words "Millionaire" and "Sha'woman" together with my brand. There is a lot of darkness in the spiritual world around money, and I have now discovered, there are also locked tight beliefs about Shamanism. I'm going to tear these apart in this chapter, with positive intention, to show you that you can access your inner Shaman too, and why you should. You can restore your spiritual power and use it for your own good and the good of humanity. You don't have to "become a Shaman", but you can arouse your inner fire and reclaim who you really are and what you're supposed to be doing here in the world. And you can make money as well.

If you wake up one day and you feel an inner knowing that you are meant for more (or if you are already sitting with this feeling)… I want to help you trust it and take your next steps along a revolutionary path of Awakened Wealth.

The world is going through a radical shift right now. I believe the pivot I made in my business to a more divine service, and the events that ran up to that are part of it. I am going to explain about how the way we see money will be a big part of the change. The Maya predicted "the birth of a new earth" centuries ago—a process of consciousness transmutation—led by the Light Leaders who surrender to the next vibrational world of experience. To do this, we must release ourselves completely from victim consciousness and release the beliefs systems that make us see polarity instead of 'just forces that exist in the universe', doing what they do. The Shaman is at peace with polarity and knows it serves a divine purpose.

There has to be balance in the universe and that begins with us breaking free from the narrow reality tunnel that comes from the projection of our trauma. When you let go of the battle you have inside, duality no longer exists and there is nothing left to prevent you from living a limitless version of life. And I believe money is a side effect of that.

In my book, *Awaken Your Miracle Frequency; It's Easier Than You Think To Have It All*, I share my own journey of doing this. I was the proverbial "hungry caterpillar" who was consuming life based on the same limited beliefs about wealth and success that have become integrated into our collective beliefs and stories, creating our very map of reality and identity. Because of that, I know that lack is only self-limitation and not truth. In order to transform into a butterfly and fly free into integrity with Divine Will and true essence, I had to literally dissolve into caterpillar slop within a chrysalis.

Unlike the caterpillar, I didn't walk into my chrysalis willingly. I experienced a tragedy that forced me there. And just like my limiting beliefs were sabotaging my freedom to live in integrity then, yours may be sabotaging you now. And if not now, they will in the future, unless you identify them and embrace your own transformation.

We are literally living through an apocalypse, in the original definition of the word, which means to "take the lid off or reveal what's been hidden" — personally and collectively.

Just like the events of the last few years have revealed, the most threatening virus on the planet is the illusion of lack, which creates the fear and limitation that lowers vibrational energy and keeps us dependent and stuck.

Now, more than ever, we need to become anchored in our true nature and unleash our immense inner power, sourced from a place that cannot be penetrated by anything outside of us. If we can do this, we can thrive through any challenge—take quantum leaps in our life and divine purpose, and become the midwives of a beautiful planetary transformation in consciousness.

That is why you are "hearing the call." That is why my Inner Shaman got noisy! We are being called collectively as the new earth energy begins to wake up new states of consciousness.

What does this have to with money and wealth?

We don't breathe oxygen because it's going to run out. We breathe it because it is a miraculous life-giving source of the energy that enables us to thrive in life, and for every breath in of oxygen we return carbon dioxide that is part of a natural cycle. Plants take up the carbon dioxide we breathe out and use it to produce the vast array of organic compounds needed for life. Why do we see money any differently?

I know you can hear the answer reverberating around your mind— "because money can run out"—and perhaps you have experienced that scarcity in your past and you feel the fear of it.

That is why money holds such a capacity to shut down power and create helplessness and that is where the world is right now, stuck in extreme polarity between helplessness and power. "The rich continue to get richer and the poor are currently poorer than they have ever been" by unconscious choice that comes from either having freedom from the beliefs that shut down power and create helplessness, or being a victim to them. I used to struggle financially and now I can see how my struggle was self-created. I was in debt, dependent on others, and not supporting anybody.

Now in a wealthier position, I pay my bills, I am dependent on myself, and I donate thousands of dollars every year to charity. And I know that's just the start.

Let's look back at the comparison I made to oxygen… is it feeling easier to swallow now? Let's swap out the word "oxygen" for "abundance." I breathe in abundance because it is a miraculous life-giving source of the energy that enables me to thrive in life, and for every breath in of abundance, I return abundance that is part of a natural cycle. Other people take up the abundance I breathe out and use it to produce the vast array of "things" needed for life.

The person stuck financially is breathing in abundance and holding their breath, wondering why they are not thriving.

And it is because of "the virus" (their illusion of lack and the fear it creates!)

This is the World War 3 we have been apprehending. Only that which kills isn't guns or bombs. It is fear.

It certainly did take a Shaman a number of years to master Divination and healing because they had to face many initiations and rites of passage that helped them let go of fear. By facing the truth of who they are, outside of the influence of their community and the collective, they could release their false ego, and be reborn with a new set of values that were more in alignment with their destiny to be of greater service to the world. 'Back in the day' these initiations involved fighting bears and being buried alive, but what if, right here and now in your life, you have been presented and are being presented with your own rites of passage? In victim consciousness, we have challenges because we are holding onto limiting stories, beliefs, fear, and bitterness. We are lost in the shadows. The collective reality constructs support us staying locked in this prison. In my book, *Awaken Your Miracle Frequency; It's Easier Than You Think To Have It All*, I talk about how I heard a podcast where the guy called this the "Victim Olympics." The premise of this is that everyone is competing to be the biggest victim and society celebrates it with all the systems set up to give people handouts and compensation. In a shift of perspective, bad circumstances seed the perfect conditions to initiate life-changing and permanent shifts in consciousness that change the course of our life. There is always light in darkness.

Back to that oxygen, holding your breath.

This is the way of the old earth. We are in a war between fear and love. Governments need us stuck in powerlessness and in fear because that is how society has been able to function for centuries. Again, in my book, I share about how I grieved the false sense of safety and security that my own powerlessness had given me. The energy of fear will only manifest more of what you fear, but if you can remove fear from your life, you will manifest a beautiful, exhilarating and abundant life easily and this will heal the polarity between helplessness and power by creating harmony. There is no harmony in those who are stuck behind the walls that they are self-creating. Taking bricks from their walls and chucking them at those who accept their rites of passage, will not free all parts of themselves into love and create a life that they love because of it. It will not enable them to share their soul gifts and talents, and breathe in abundance because of that. As a Coach, I see many other coaches tied to virtual stakes to burn like witches because their clients feel burned by their services. However, a coach can only be a midwife to their client's transformation. As the saying goes… you can lead a horse to water, but ultimately the horse has to put their head down to the water, hang their tongue out, and drink. Some people just won't. Victim consciousness runs deep. And I think it's sad because, personally, I'm celebrating every Light Warrior that chooses to get up every morning, create self-sufficiency and try and change the world in a positive way. We can do this simply by continuing to focus on shifting our own vibration. I think we should be lifting them up because when you meet yourself and your walls over and over again, in life or in business, and you choose to overcome them so you expand and grow, you are helping to win this war between love and fear. We won't win it by fighting. So how do we take a journey through the collective fear of the old earth paradigm, which is entrenched in society, and find our way back to the love that will be the oxygen of the new earth?

Not to understate… the Shaman's heart is FEARLESS. There is too much fear in the collective. Much of the "brick throwing" from people criticising those creating wealth is projection of the fear that stems from their deep inner turmoil. This is taking away their personal power and creating the helplessness that is causing them to depend on the hierarchical power structures they profess to hate. To heal fear, you must take a deep healing journey. I show you how you can do this in my book, so you gain the flexibility of mind to let go of the ideas you hold onto, exactly like, "the poor are getting poorer and the richer getting richer." That is, in fact, programming, not truth, and it's driven by the perception of lack that is fed to us from all directions—the media, education, policy, etc. A powerful question to keep asking is... Why?

One of the first concepts I was introduced to as I stepped onto the Shaman's path was the principle of exchange that has always been active between the giver and receiver of healing and wisdom. Obviously, what was exchanged looked very different depending on the time you look at in history, the geography of the exchange and what was considered valuable, but nothing has ever been given for free. In the past, you might have been exchanging your spiritual gifts for a potato rather than a dollar! This aligns with the Law of the Universe too—everything is in flow and at every level of universal existence, harmony is achieved through exchange. How does that apply to today's world and money? Money is the thing that holds the most value in terms of exchange. Money is currently the vehicle to lodging, food, and comfort. I saw a Shaman's website once that talked about how he gave all his stuff away for free, then he had a "Gift Page." Because people should understand that in this day and age it is not possible for him to live for free and so a suggested donation could be offered for each service. My mind was blown by this. "Begging" is better than exchanging value for value? This is at the heart of the problem of spiritual leaders giving their stuff away for free. They are self-limiting themselves behind the wall of helplessness because they are unwilling to see money in a different way. Money is ultimately the end form in matter of energy, influenced by how we see it based on our beliefs. Like everything else in the universe. This is Quantum Physics. This method of exchange is also evolving, as cryptocurrencies are being seen to hold higher value, because of their accessibility to all and other reasons. For a time, this digital currency was talked down by banks and governments and we were warned of scams and risks. Now those who threw the rocks are busy trying to gain ground on holding the power over these currencies because now their take up is a risk to the old way of money. For a minute window, we have the opportunity to influence how cryptocurrencies go forward, in the hands of people, if we find our power to lead with light in our perceptions and actions, and use our voices to guide how the new earth collective reality is constructed. However, most are too busy fighting to stay behind the walls of their own self limits because this is the place where they feel safest. And from this position of powerlessness, we stand to risk another world of vibrational experience coming from lack and fear programming because we won't stop the birth of a New World Order. The contractions have already started. I have had to have my own evolution in programming to reach a position where I am ready to lead with light into this New World. For a time, I confused "harmony" with the old-world paradigm of "love", feeling as if you could give infinite amounts of it, infinitely. Only this is outside the natural order of the Universe as well. It is the opposite of the breath that is held in fear and is the exhale that forgets to breathe in and so perishes equally. In a natural rhythm of in breath and out breath we thrive. Love harvests because lack can't exist in this (L)evel (O)f (V)ibrational (E)nergy[1]. And as I discovered, the resistance to breathe back in love comes down to a deep lack of self-worth and undeserving and a vibration of lack that creates problems instead of solving them.

The thing that I am sure of now, having had the blessing to hang out in both extremes of polarity, is that a struggling population is a dependent population. In a chat with a friend around my ideas for this chapter, she said, regarding the message from my ex-client that I began this chapter with… "I can see where she is coming from… The rich are getting richer, at least here in America. In America, the rich people have gotten richer and richer, and richer, and richer. And it's understandable because income hasn't gone up for people in regular jobs. It's only increased about 10% or 15% since Reagan was President, which means it hasn't gone up in equation with everything to do with the cost of living, like buying a house for less than a ridiculous amount of money or even rent-

---

1   (L)evel (Of) (V)ibrational (E)nergy - LOVE is not a concept that is
     mine, but a concept from my breathwork mentor, Niraj Naik

ing. Everything's gone up, except if you work at McDonald's. Then you're still going to make $8 or $9 an hour."

A question that came straight to me was this… Who is setting the minimum wage and what would be the benefit in one of the most powerful countries in the world, to keeping the minimum wage low in a society as we know it that survives off the polarity between helplessness and power?

(In Belgium, you can apparently make $22 an hour, have full employment benefits and health benefits…)

The answer is slavery, and it is accepted and even supported because from the position of the majority, in the polarity of helplessness, this looks like a system that provides security and safety. Society is hypnotized by the promise of our leaders to solve our problems for us, instead of us waking up to the true power and potential hidden beneath our deep-rooted unworthiness and generational trauma.

And in our unwillingness to let go of the programs and things we hold onto, and be open to the hope of a better way, the light diminishes. This is the classic case of the oxygen mask. If the oxygen does disappear… grab for your own oxygen mask first. Because filled back up with the miraculous, life-giving source of the energy that enables us to thrive in life, you can save others.

What I see in Light Leaders, Lightworkers and Starseeds is the same as my story. A microscopic step forward in their healing and then they want, from the good in their hearts, to go out and shine their light to others. However, they are only able to shine their light with a torch, instead of becoming a Lighthouse. My own progress was non-existent to slow when I was blind to the beliefs that were limiting me and my resistance to have someone shine their light on my situation. My rejection of their offer of assistance came from the constant belief "I couldn't afford it". When I shattered this limiting paradigm, I began my journey to become a Lighthouse. Not immediately. There were rites of passage to move through (and certainly there had been rites of passage I had already moved through). My point is that the evolution was ever unfolding and the more I fuelled my Lighthouse with healing, the brighter my light shone and the further its impact reached. Healing has a ripple effect. Are we sacrificing the potential for a galactivation of healing because of what we're not willing to let go of and the fears we are unwilling to face?

There are certainly a million Light Leaders, Light Workers, and Starseeds out there right now and lots of them aren't making any money at all. Can we correlate entrenched money programming that is negative to this block in the natural cycle of giving abundance and receiving abundance in return because so many are holding their breath in fear?

I began working with a new client in January 2023. She came to my in-person retreat in Mexico and it was a magickal experience. She had an Awakening at the event as to the disharmony in her inner world and decided to continue working with me after the event. She described my Neurosomatic Expansion Retreat like "entering a Portal of Truth." Six months on, her whole world has changed. She is speaking on stages, booked for TEDx, and reaching nearly 100k people with her social media content. She puts the shift down to the consistency and value that was activated by her removing her inner blocks. She no longer feels like an imposter. She has been able to birth her truth, message, voice, and the impact that was her soul goal. However, this client has been consistently late with payments. Her invoice would become overdue every month and we would have to reach out about the money owed. One day I asked her outright, "what's going on"? She admitted that she had a pattern of holding onto money because in her past experiences, with both her parents and her ex-partner, they had control of her money. She was holding onto money because it made her feel secure. I asked her if she was seeing money come in from her increased reach and opportunities and her answer was, no. I told her that was crazy. She could see my methods working to attract clients, could she believe that the block was her block, energetically, to do with money, that was stopping the conversion to getting paid? I challenged her to start letting money go and see if this shifted her financial flow. Within one week it had! At the end of the day, we all have the same amount of creative power, so we can put ourselves wherever we want to be when we let go of the reasons that we keep ourselves where we are. Biologically, we actually need to let go of fear to access our creative mind, also known as superconsciousness! And that's what the Shaman masters too. They learn how to access their Ultramind and the divine assistance that is available to anyone who is willing to release fear. This altered state of consciousness is where they employ the shamanic traditions they use to heal. It's the pay-off for finding their lion's heart. Which means that gift is available to you too. We all have access to the gift of healing and divination. I want to wake up that power in everybody because it is part of making the choice in every moment to choose love over fear, which will heal the world as our frequency rises because at that level of vibrational energy, problems disappear. My story proves it. In *Awaken Your Miracle Frequency; It's Easier Than You Think To Have It All*, I share multiple stories that will blow your mind and help you trust that as your frequency rises, life aligns around you. Amidst this process, it can feel like things are falling apart! I know that when I heard the call of my Inner Shaman, it felt like my life was in total chaos. I felt like I had business depression! I had made the big decision to pivot my business and follow this inner compass that was directing me into the unknown. I was literally just following my nose and taking action as inspiration came to me. For the first time in forever, I had no plan, and it felt epic. I decided to do a live launch of a new low-ticket programme I had designed in this creative wave of chaos, which was successful, but someone also ended up signing up as a 1:1 client as well. She came from an event I had done before I pivoted my business. As we began to onboard her and she learned more about my new "Awakened Wealth Blueprint," she became "allergic" to my approach to making money. She had come from a corporate background where it wouldn't make sense to her that she could make money without hustling for it. She spoke of my lean towards Law Of Attraction and Manifestation like I was selling snake oil. This "allergic reaction" to my new way of working led to her say some shitty things in her emails about my credibility and price point that didn't feel good. Although I didn't believe them… right then and there, my front-facing marketing and branding was a thorn in my side. I couldn't get away from the idea of becoming "The Millionaire Sha'woman" and helping people make money by healing their past trauma and awakening their creative power (whilst regenerating forests and making good on that promise I made to my spirit animals!!!!) However, I had this MASSIVE block about showing this reinvention of myself to the world. This led me, a couple of months later, to sign up to a Shaman School. My hopes in this decision were to understand how I answer this call from my Inner Shaman, understand the call and what I was experiencing, and understand how I go forward. I was surprised when I started the programme. I saw how I wasn't really being taught anything. I was being shown a way to find my way within myself. And what I understand now, nearly a year down the line, is that if you don't learn how to listen to your inner voice, you can't follow it, and you won't end up anywhere. So, as crazy as the voice sounds, LISTEN. It is your Waiata O Te Wairua (soul's song) calling the lost parts of your soul home. I heard this song in the trees down in my local reserve, one day as I was walking and pondering my steps forward with this yearning deep within to go in a new direction. The trees seemed to be singing, "Wai." For Māori, wai holds mauri—a spiritual life force and I realised I was being urged to follow my heart. Just like the water flows without direction, I simply had to become fluid to the direction of my next steps. Seven months into my Shaman School, I was introduced to a New Zealand Teacher Plant called Red Matipo. It is the plant that supports the targeted work of calling lost parts of the soul home. Scattered, fragmented, lost, and traumatized parts of our soul get frozen in time and it is the Shaman's role to retrieve them, in order to restore seed potential. The Shaman has to travel deep into the belly of the great Mother, the underworld to do this. For me, this has been the most challenging rite of passage yet, as a Shaman, travelling back to retrieve the parts of my own soul that departed in the moments of my childhood and a past life that were simply too overwhelming. I had no idea how this process would be so intricately connected to my business growth and particularly, scaling my income. So yes, in some ways it's provocative to put "Millionaire" and "Sha'woman" together in a sentence, but challenging people's ways of thinking will lead to conversations that will free people. The Soul is the vital breath that activates life in our human form.

I remember how quite recently, one of my own QuNtum Leap Master Coaches was triggered by a post on social media where I acknowledged myself as a shaman. Someone had told her that Shamans were humble and free of ego. It struck me how sad it is that acknowledging your desire to help others with your soul work and making that pledge publicly could be seen as something egoic instead of impactful, just because of what you might call yourself. Especially considering that you do not choose the path of Shaman. It chooses you. And it often follows tragedy like I experienced, which becomes the Shaman's first step in overcoming the negative powers of death and disease and healing others with empathy. I have had some wild experiences since answering "yes" to the call of my Inner Shaman. I haven't talked openly about most of them because most people are just too fixed in their belief systems to understand them. I have had two near death experiences; I was visited repeatedly over a number of nights in two different locations by the lost soul of a client who kept waking me up by screaming "mum" in my face. What was crazy about that was when I mentioned it to my husband, he'd had the same experience on one of the nights. Like the soul was simply searching for someone to hear it. When we made the breakthrough with my client, the nocturnal screaming stopped. I have also had multiple out of body journeys that move between being terrifying and beautiful and I now believe that accessing Superconsciousness in this way is the magick of the new earth that is birthing, and potential that is available to every Light Leader, Light Worker, and Starseed to navigate their business in a new way. This is the way to feel fully aligned, have radical and beautiful expression of your soul gifts, and the greatest potential for income, impact, and influence with maximum ease, joy, and freedom. Experiencing this expanded version of your life unfold from you is what I call awakening a Miracle Frequency that ensures a beautiful and continuing cycle of abundance. I created the Awakened Wealth Blueprint so that you have a path to burst the false containers within which you limit yourself and your mythic potential, to realise your inner power and unleash your freedom of choice and creativity. Otherwise, you will always be a robot to the beliefs that enable the divide between helplessness and power.

When you can breakthrough where you are not willing to feel VULNERABLE to what you fear, you will breakthrough to your next level of income as well. What does this look like for you?

- Is it where you are afraid to "get it wrong" in your business?
- Is it where you are afraid to "not be perfect"?
- Is it where you are afraid to "get into trouble"?
- Is it where you are afraid to "get hurt"?
- Is it where you are afraid to "be humiliated", or feel other uncomfortable feelings that scarred you as a child?

Ask yourself right now, how is this showing up in your business?

- Not charging your **WORTH**?
- Not asking for the **SALE**?
- Not being creatively **EXPRESSED**?
- Over-control, over-thinking and over-**WORKING**?
- Feeling misaligned in your **MARKETING**?
- Issues with payments and **CLIENTS**?
- Income rollercoasters, or struggling to breakthrough a certain income **PLATEAU**?

You are attracting every situation you have in your business and life from the insecurity, doubt and fear you have. So likely, you will see the above come in frustrating and repeating patterns.

If you are ready to liberate yourself from these limits, so you can explore your light, have radical expression and follow your star trail, I am ready to support you.

However, I'm not the Coach for your Victim's Story.

You must want **CHANGE**. You must be willing to awaken your lion's heart and step into your **MYSTERY**!

Alternatively, enjoy life as a robot.

Overflow will always come when you overcome. When you swap fighting, forcing, and resisting for ease, surrender, and trust in the opportunities for **EXPANSION** that you are currently being gifted, but confusing for "curveballs," challenges, and 'life happening'. When you begin the journey of Awakened Wealth and as you Awaken your Miracle Frequency, the Universe will only show you the easiest way and your **FEELINGS**—especially fear—are the key to your transformative power. Your emerging reality will come from your continuing expansion in consciousness and more creativity, money, and abundance will overflow when you can switch off your conscious mind. It is the **KRYPTONITE** to your Superconscious Powers! Your next mastery is releasing your unconscious fears and learning to use this ultramind to invite ease, bliss, and inner-sight into how you run your business and live your life.

If you are ready to take that journey, I am ready to be your Shaman. I feel able to say that now; I acknowledge my path in the collective dreamfield as a midwife of planetary transformation, for quantum healing and transducing. I made my conscious break with the past and created a new relationship with the future. I am consciously choosing to play and be played in the game of the Greater Reality, so I can continue to free into love any areas of separation, pain, fear, denial, judgment or limitation in my being. You can do the same.

Humanity is at a crossroads. Elon Musk is quoted to have said, "The biggest issue in 20 years will be population **COLLAPSE**, not explosion." It's time for Light Leaders to step the fuck up and **EMBODY** the essence of truth. There is no lack, there is no uncertainty, everything we have is coming from us, and it's time to use our **GIFTS** to swing the pendulum back to harmony, an elixir for the poisons of helplessness and power and a cure to the virus creating the fear that is crippling us. That starts **WITHIN US**. We have created a monster, but it is not outside of us, like we have been taught to believe. The unconscious unsafety of the average human being's energy body **RUNS DEEP** and it will require a Somatic Evolution to heal. My book, *Awaken Your Miracle Frequency; It's Easier Than You Think To Have It All*, can be your guide and a tool on how to heal, release, grow, and believe that the impossible really is possible, whatever your circumstances have been in life. You will understand how to tap into the Quantum Field through a higher consciousness that will literally save the world, and fully embrace the vulnerability of everything you fear about living into your deepest potential. You will find your wings and begin to fly on the current of your dreams, full of joy, happiness, and a ripple effect of healing that washes over the world through your impact.

We are, in fact, living at a beautiful time where access to those who need us the most is at our fingertips, thanks to the internet, but you have to stop playing down parts of yourself, catch attention to be seen and heard because the online space is so crowded (and will become impossible to penetrate with the tide of AI!) The ideas, innovation, and expression that will STAND OUT and create the Movement you want will channel easily through your Superconscious mind, and I am excited to teach you how to access it and activate your Light Body.

If you are the girl or guy with a Millionaire Sha'Man or Woman inside you, a story inside you, wisdom beyond lifetimes, and you are hearing the call, receive my invitation to take a deeper journey of healing, exploration of possibility and spiritual leadership. You are ready for the journey of Awakened Wealth and my book, *Awaken Your Miracle Frequency; It's Easier Than You Think To Have It All* is the roadmap to your next steps from here to give up the old paradigm of business built on force and control, lean into a New Earth Frequency and let your heart become your compass. You don't need more strategy. You are ready for your Mystery. You can access this at https://www.awakenedwealthblueprint.com/mf_book I'm excited to meet you there!

Vicky 'Sparkle' Leckenby

Transformational and trauma-informed coach for Light-leaders, supporting visionaries and healers to unleash their full potential. Vicky has trained in various modalities and transformational coaching methods to combine the necessary inner work with the business strategy to assist others in aligning to their soul purpose.

Diamond in the Rough

Revealing the Many Facets of the Self-Worth Journey

by Vicky 'Sparkle' Leckenby

"The soul is placed in the body like a rough diamond, and must be polished, or the lustre of it will never appear."
—DANIEL DEFOE

This is a story of a Soul's Journey of Self-Worth. The journey of my own soul and the journey of the soul reading this right now, you.

Today, my "diamond" of self-worth is shining, sparkling, more brightly than ever. Its brilliance has touched all areas of my life so I now experience the abundance that flows from that.

I live from my mantra, "Choose You," understanding that I always have a choice to either confirm or undermine my self-worth in every moment and with each decision.

In the beginning, my inner self-worth diamond started out raw, a diamond in the rough. I hid my light and "chose others" over self.

My journey, which I suspect like yours, has been an uncovering and polishing of the differing "facets" of that diamond of self-worth, so that its beauty, sparkle, and light reflected my outer reality. I call it my "inner sparkle," that light that, once ignited, cascades out firework style and touches everyone and everything.

I have learned that everything in our lives, including our businesses, is a reflection of our internal self-worth diamond.

As I have polished each "facet" revealed to me, my external reality has shifted. I want to share with you the most crucial facets of my own diamond in the order of how they showed up for me. In doing so, it is my hope that your own Self Worth Diamond may shine brighter. Ultimately, we all take a unique path so perhaps for you, there's a different sequence to which your diamond's facets are polished and when. This is perfect because no two diamonds are the same.

> *"Better to be a diamond in the rough,*
> *than a polished fake in denial."*
> —T.F HODGE

At almost 50, my own self-worth was hidden way under the rubble for the large majority of my life. My ability to value myself was so low that the light permeating outwards from my inner diamond lacked "authentic sparkle." It was more like a cubic zirconia, the pretend diamond; shiny and sparkly at first glance, but once you put it under a microscope, a clear fake.

Like many of us, I grew up in an environment where I was praised for being the good girl. I was good at school, good at singing and dancing, and very good at being useful. Not only did this good girl behaviour give me a feeling of validation, it kept me safe—well, mostly!

I have one brother, and he was the complete opposite! He got into trouble, got dirty and hated schoolwork. More than not conforming, he was openly defiant. The result was regular and severe beatings! My conclusion was that if I kept my head down and fell in line, I could avoid the painful consequences that my brother endured. This strategy worked to some extent, but it was not a fool-proof plan and sometimes the punishment came anyway.

As a result, my nervous system was hardwired to be in a state of high alert—the type of hypervigilance you'd expect from a security camera triggered by a cat or leaves blowing by. I watched for signs of danger like some kind of soldier on lookout duty, prepared for action in any given moment.

It was my normal state of being, and I became accustomed to it throughout school, university and into my adult life. The programme was so deeply imprinted into the blueprint of the book of life that it was silently copied from page to page undetected. Through this way of being, I lost almost all sense of who I was. Mask upon mask protected me to the point of not even realising those masks were there. My survival instinct was so strong that I managed to delude myself. My inner diamond of authenticity and being able to accept myself was buried under layers and layers of protection, a real diamond in the rough replaced by a fake substitute and I didn't even know.

"I've always been right here buried under the rubble of fear; I simply forgot how near I've always been to the heart that holds love dear."
—LUCY MARY BALL

I started my professional work life as a Business and Economics teacher. In this role, I used my well-honed chameleon-like abilities to charm and impress my superiors. Promotions came quickly, and I climbed the ladder of outward success. Unfortunately, this success came at a huge cost! I worked insane hours and lived on adrenaline in a state of panic. It required ridiculous amounts of energy to keep all those masks in place and look like I had it all together. Still, I prided myself on my ability to produce outstanding results. To uphold my Miss Efficiency status, I was unable to say no to my colleagues. Everyone knew that you could count on Vicky to get the job done! For this reason, I had to shift jobs every three years to start with a clean slate in a new school, owing to the sheer weight of my ever-expanding workload.

You'd think that taking a break to be a full-time mum to my two under twos would shed some light on my patterns, right? Unfortunately, no! I turned into Superwomen putting myself under incredible pressure to get it right! True to form, in the mum's groups, I repeated the pattern, putting my hand up in those awkward silences when no one else wanted to.

By this point, I'd moved away from the U.K. and to a new life in New Zealand, and I had begun to have some awareness of my inability to say no and my tendency to people please in exchange for approval. In meetings, I would actually sit on my hands to prevent one of them from being thrust in the air to take on some unwanted task.

The reality was that as a full-time mum, I was even busier than before. Everyone who needed an ear got one. Everyone who needed a favour got it. I was completely worn out. I read books about boundaries but even though I knew what I was doing, I still said yes anyway.

Like the heat and pressure required to form a diamond, it seemed I needed even more pressure to unlock my authentic voice.

I was in a horribly toxic marriage and tolerating incessant criticism and unacceptable treatment. I told lies to avoid conflict most days. My head felt like it would spin trying to remember the details of what I'd previously said. Then, there were the times I'd get caught. Shame, disgust, and anger followed detracting me from any ability to accept myself.

It wasn't only in my marriage that the pressure was on. I'd started a skincare and makeup business from home so I could be with the kids and continue my quest for the title of mother of the year. Only now I had a whole team of beauty consultants to manage and with my poor boundaries, I created a monster where most of them depended heavily on me. I made myself available 24/7 and cared more about their success than they did.

My hubby approached this new development with a dual pressure tactic. First, he stopped working and took over the homeschooling of our kids so I could focus on my business and pull in the expected finances, the overseas reward trips, and extra gifts I managed to achieve. Second, he complained about my poor boundaries and how it impacted the family, constantly criticising me. To make money, I felt like I had no choice but to hustle hard. It was a no-win scenario, and I told lies everywhere to keep control.

FACET ONE – CHOOSING ME THROUGH UNLOCKING MY AUTHENTIC VOICE

I remember so clearly the day it got to be too much and I handed in my Supermum badge. I finally admitted I couldn't do it anymore, that the finances were a mess, that he needed to go back to work, and that I needed to run my business part-time. All the lying had left me feeling worthless, and I vowed to begin to tell the truth, however difficult.

I started with the little things. "No, I'm staying home tonight, it's been a big week" instead of some story of why I couldn't go to dinner with friends. "I hit the snooze button and fell back asleep" instead of stories about how unbelievable the traffic had been.

You see, these little excuses are really justified lies that have become acceptable in society. I mean who really believes anyone when there was yet another crash on your way to work for the third time that week?

What I realised was that even if I was fooling others, I could never fool myself. Ultimately, I knew I was a liar and right there was my first invitation to choose me and unlock the first facet of my self-worth diamond!

After all, I hated it when I found other people to be liars! I didn't trust them or like them after discovering that. It was with this that I realised this integrity piece was the cornerstone of improving my self-esteem. I saw how each time I had told a lie/excuse to either impress, avoid disapproval or unwanted consequences, I had chosen to place the opinions of others over my own opinion of myself.

This was such a huge revelation! It became a no compromise, zero tolerance way to live. I drew a line in the sand that I would not rob from my own pot of self-validation. It became obvious to me how I had been trapped on the treadmill of being addicted to external validation.

Every time I had said yes, when I had wanted to say no, I'd taken from my pot. Every time, I'd told an excuse, I'd taken from my pot. Every time I'd done or said anything not congruent with my truth, I'd taken from my pot.

The result of all this taking from the pot of internal validation meant that the temptation to seek external validation to fill the void was irresistible.

The pot was like a bucket with holes in the bottom. External validation in, internal validation out. I was like an addict and for me, my rehabilitation method was cold turkey style truth. What was incredible is that with each truth, I felt the holes in my bucket healing. Each time I told the truth when it was uncomfortable, it was a vote for me! A celebration of choosing me that felt so strong that sometimes I did a happy dance with the acknowledgement of this new way to be. It was like building muscles and with every win, I got stronger until I was confronted with the realisation that my integrity with others was one thing but what about the stories I had been telling myself?

This radical level of honesty led to me finally shifting out of victimhood and being a martyr, to taking self-responsibility in a way I'd never done before. Honestly, I felt so empowered that my self-esteem rocketed, and I realised I'd stumbled upon something universal.

Around this same time, I also came to understand that my lack of integrity had also been hiding another deeply ingrained pattern—that of feeling responsible for other's feelings. I'd feel super guilty if I thought my truth would either cause someone else pain, discomfort or inconvenience. I protected people from the truth based on a story I projected onto them. Pretty insulting really and not giving others much credit.

I realised that my only responsibility was to be in integrity. That I was not responsible for how the other person interpreted my truth if it was delivered with good intentions. Finally, being able to distinguish between what belonged to me and what didn't, together with my rising self-esteem, over time, these feelings of responsibility lost their grip on me.

This has transformed how I operate not only as a human, but in business. It is excruciating watching someone conduct a sales call without this piece in place. Without your authentic voice, it is impossible to stand up and declare your authority in your field of expertise which is crucial to whether your audience trusts that you can help them or not. Not to mention, how could I possibly coach others if I couldn't call out uncomfortable truths when needed?

Every single facet here, every single personal revelation has had huge ramifications for my work as a Light Worker and Coach.

FACET 2 – CHOOSING ME THROUGH LOVE

A consequence of this elevated self-worth is that I reached the point of knowing I had to leave my marriage. I attempted to put in boundaries, but they were not met with respect, and so, after 13 years together, we parted ways. Reflecting on how I'd got myself into such a mess in the first place, it led me to examining the second facet of my self-worth diamond.

I knew that my responsibility had been in what I'd allowed and tolerated. I admitted to myself that there were some co-dependent behaviours going on. Namely, the superhero fixer behaviour, together with being a martyr, that had given me years of sustenance of being the victim and feeling needed. What a great distraction! I hadn't had to look at my own flaws for years because I'd been so focused on his!

I was simply deluded in my role of being a good wife whilst internally blaming him for everything that was wrong. Secretly seething inside, smiling on the outside and somehow still believing I was the angel in this situation. I called bullshit on myself and realised I was anything but nice. I don't say this to shame but to be direct. This is one component of the kind of fakery which destroys relationships.

So there, I had it—my new revelation that my entire blueprint for what it is to love was a disaster. It was clear to me that until I tackled this, I could not undertake a healthy relationship romantically.

I journalled about what I thought love was and what I knew it wasn't. It's so interesting to realise where we inherit our love blueprints from. In my case, from divorced parents, which is pretty standard these days, and also from songs and movies that scream toxicity. I grew up listening to "I can't live if living is without you" and "Everything I do, I do it for you!" Yikes!

Don't even get me started on Disney and the teenage romance novels I used to read. For me, starring in my own romcom in real life had been the expectation. Knight in shining armour, white picket fence, happily ever after. I decided that "Disney Vicky" needed a reality check.

My journal of "what it is to love" now contained statements about respect, trust and acceptance. I wrote out a list of my new expectations (standards) about how I would be loved. I resolved to accept nothing less or stay single. It immediately dawned on me that if I wanted to be loved to this standard, I must be prepared to give love the same way. I rewrote the list again; this time as a list of promises about how I would love others. Yet, this process was still not complete. That's right, how could I expect anyone else to give me what I couldn't first give myself? That gave rise to my third and final list, a list of my declaration of how I would, from this day forward, choose to love myself.

On each list, acceptance featured at the top. To me, to love is to really accept the other in a way that we give unconditional love to a child. As a parent, whatever they might do or say, they are loved. The end. We might not have all experienced that but it's what we all want. To be loved is to be fully seen, heard and accepted.

So, I embarked on radical self-acceptance. Turns out that with integrity, this process is much easier when you can operate in authenticity and drop those masks because it means that you can feel good about yourself.

I can report that this decision to take responsibility to choose to love me transformed my external relationships beyond all recognition. Beautiful new friends entered my life and any remnants of my toxic past disappeared. Not one single "taker" remained. Soon after, I met Pablo. A true gentleman who meets me at my standard. I feel free, accepted and well-loved, without the kind of toxic attachment that coloured my previous relationships.

When I chose to rewrite my blueprint for love, it was from a place of "no more" and a position of being prepared to stay single. That new standard was about me and what I knew I deserved and my commitment to give that love to me. I realised that the external manifestation of this standard was evidence of healing my relationship with myself. This proved to be another crucial insight— not to chase the external, but to seek it first within. The evidence of that internal transformation is what shows up in the mirror like magic.

FACET 3 – CHOOSING ME THROUGH MY PHYSICAL APPEARANCE

It's interesting to me that my journey of self-acceptance was one that started on the inside first. For many others, it is the opposite. For me, I was able to say I liked myself on the inside well in advance of my struggle to like what I saw in the mirror.

From an early age, aesthetics were highly valued by my family, in particular by my father. Growing up in the U.K. with such an emphasis on makeup and fashion, your appearance almost seemed like it determined the measure of a person. At that time, we had the waif-like Kate Moss gracing the catwalk and the pressure to be body beautiful exploded. With the rise of social media in recent years, I feel for my daughter's generation, growing up in a world of airbrushing, photo filters and butt implants.

As kids, my brother and I stayed in our lanes. Him in sports and me in academia. We didn't switch lanes which resulted in him not finishing school and me not being very active. I wasn't even big but in comparison, I felt huge! My diet was awful too! Mum left our family when I was 12, and I was free to eat as much sugar as I wanted. I developed a very unhealthy relationship with food, particularly, with sugar. Never allowing my weight to get out of control and yo-yo-ing in weight between summer and winter became the norm. In my 20s, I would almost starve myself and be at the gym constantly for a couple of months prior to bikini time, only to return and pile it all back on over the winter, hiding under baggy jumpers.

It hasn't helped that I've worked in the beauty industry. My levels of vanity reached new heights. I often needed to hop online to promote products, but I was scared to be judged for not having the right look. Oftentimes, I would avoid being online because it was just too much effort to get ready or because I was at the wrong end of my yo-yo weight cycle.

This vanity and lack of accepting my appearance kept me small in my business for other reasons too. How is it possible to develop a personal brand without photos? I'd put off photo shoots to some future point when I imagined I'd look better. The only problem with this strategy was that I was getting older, so I had a new issue—I needed more makeup to keep the self-talk at bay! Another mask, but a visible one. I hated being caught without makeup by unexpected visitors and would run off to the bathroom to apply a quick "fix"!

Finally, I couldn't bear it anymore, and I was ready to tackle this area of self-worth. I didn't want to be held back anymore by this. I'd tried to change things before; some things I'd been successful with, so there were clues there. The areas I'd stuck to were when my resolve for a lifestyle change was firm and not from a temporary bikini goal. I'd become vegetarian and had no problems maintaining my position with zero temptation. Why? I had made an identity shift. Same with gluten. I adopted a gluten-free lifestyle to avoid the inevitable painful symptoms.

Again, I drew another line in the sand to live by a new standard. This time, it wasn't based on what I wanted to look like but on how I wanted to feel. A commitment to giving my body the nourishment it needs to feel energetic by avoiding things that left me feeling terrible. A decision to ensure that I got enough sleep so I could enjoy my days more! I practiced breathwork to create the good feelings and the spaciousness I'm deserving of. These were just some of the new choices that aligned with that new standard. Again, it's a conscious choosing of self. Choosing what serves me in the long term over short-term gratification, which would inevitably leave me feeling worse, knowing that addiction won over self.

For me, it's been no surprise that it has happened in this order. I needed to have the other facets in place in social situations and to use my voice to decline food and beverages when everyone else was consuming sugary treats or alcohol and not be concerned about fitting in.

My self-worth celebrations are off the charts now that I am choosing me. I feel great and just like with the other areas, my focus was not on the external results, but rather the nourishing of my body and for the standard of health I want to experience. This has led to a dramatic transformation on the external.

Finally accepting and loving my external appearance has freed me in so many areas but particularly in my business where I am no longer hiding and I show up without fear to be seen. It was a big day when I went live first thing in the morning barefaced, unshowered, and in my PJs!

I can't stress how much this area of self-worth has the potential to hold us back from playing full out, especially in our work. It's sneaky too as we don't always know it's the real culprit. This fear of being visible and judged, more often than not, presents as procrastination and distraction. Sound familiar?

FACET 4 – CHOOSING ME THROUGH EMOTIONAL RELEASE AND INTEGRATION

I'd moved into a new level of vulnerability by allowing myself to be both heard and seen, both on the internal and external, yet another facet was ready to be revealed.

I heard the call of my inner children and past generations wanting to be witnessed. I had attempted inner child and past life healing before but having been emotionally numb as a coping mechanism since childhood, it wasn't experienced somatically. I helped others to release theirs but there was gnawing grief and sadness inside of me that I'd not confronted. So many of us have been conditioned to hide our pain and throughout my life I'd considered myself lucky as during my adulthood I had dodged losing anyone close to me.

Around 11 years ago, I got pregnant for the third time, and I was overjoyed. I went to my 12-week scan with my then hubby and my 3- and 4-year-old. I was so excited to see their little faces as they saw their new sibling on the screen. As the screen brought up the image of my baby, I saw a perfectly formed wee one. I knew my sonographer though, and as I looked at her face, I saw that something was very wrong. It must've been difficult for her to tell me that my baby's heart had stopped beating, probably one week prior. I was in total shock.

Nowhere in my mind had I ever imagined this scenario! I'd had no problems in my previous pregnancies, and I didn't know anyone else who'd miscarried or so I thought. I remember covering my teary eyes with my hands and asking the kid's dad to take them out of the room; I didn't want them to see their mummy fall apart, and I honestly didn't believe it.

I even went and paid for another sonogram for a second opinion.

They were performing a D&C on me and couldn't stand the thought that there was even a 0.0000001% chance that the procedure might harm a baby that might be still okay. Acceptance is a difficult process. For the week in between finding out and the procedure, I was in a weird holding pattern. I knew my baby was still inside my tummy, so, I would hold it and think about what they would have looked like.

I'd run my fingers through my kids' hair and think about how I wouldn't ever touch theirs. I'd hear my kids giggling and think about how I wouldn't get to hear their voice and their laughter. My now ex-hubby had no empathy for this.

His perspective was, well, it's happened, just move on!

I think in this fast-paced world it is typical to stuff down and repress your emotions regarding pain but for me that was actually the beginning of the end of our marriage, even way back then, as I very much felt alone emotionally. I was left feeling like I was being self-indulgent in my grieving process.

We moved to a new town shortly after, and I begged to try again because I felt like maybe a baby would be healing—like maybe another chance for this little soul to incarnate. I got pregnant immediately and this time, I went to the scan early at 9 weeks as I was terrified. As a lay on the bed, I told the sonographer what had happened and my fears of it happening again. She reassured me and began the scan. No way! Exactly the same. No heartbeat. I'd missed this one by a week again! I wasn't in the same shock as the first time, but the wave of grief hit me with massive force!

This time, it came with thoughts about what was wrong with me? Had I done something to cause this? Our brains are always seeking to make sense of our pain. Again, I felt alone in my sadness. My ex said that was the last time, that my eggs were just too old. I was 38. So, part of the grieving was the knowing that there would be no more children for me.

Of course, logically I knew I was lucky to have my beautiful children, Harvey and Lyla, and that so many women experience this and haven't any other children. I was and am truly thankful for that.

However, it doesn't mean you're exempt from the pain whatsoever! When I started to share this with friends of mine, one by one, many admitted they had also experienced a miscarriage. I was stunned to find this out. How did I not know this about some of my closest friends? It's almost taboo. Like there's shame in it. Like somehow, we are almost incomplete as women by this experience. We shouldn't live through our pain in silence.

So, fast forward to recent years, during a womb healing, I experienced a deep outpouring of repressed grief. I witnessed the pain and horror of generations passed and all that they had endured. For me, this opened up a portal back to my emotions and the feelings that, just like my voice and my appearance, had been hiding in the shadows, too afraid to come out.

I decided that abandoning myself emotionally was no longer an option and this led me to realise that my key to even greater authenticity about choosing me, included being fully integrated with all my inner children. It was then that I allowed those painful trapped emotions out.

I often receive songs as messages, and immediately after meeting with my scared and abandoned inner child to release her childhood pain, I heard these words from *The Long and Winding Road*:

> *Many times, I've been alone*
> *And many times, I've cried*
> *Anyway, you'll never know*
> *The many ways I've tried*
> *And still, they lead me back*
> *To the long winding road*
> *You left me standing here*
> *A long, long time ago*
> *Don't leave me waiting here*
> *Lead me to your door*

For me, these are HER words, the words of my little girl... the one who felt she couldn't risk being authentic. The one I abandoned who had been waiting for me to get her along the very long and winding road of over four decades and carry her in my heart.

Again, there is huge relevance to business and abundance here. What we feel, with our emotions are what bring about manifestation. Allowing these feelings to move through us liberate those trapped deep inside, which is a necessary step to creation. If we leave this in the shadows, we can only partly shine as human beings. We can put our foot down firmly on the accelerator but unfortunately our other foot is slammed on the brakes.

FACET 5 – CHOOSING ME THROUGH MY RELATIONSHIP WITH MONEY

If there's one thing I'm sure of, it's that we're never finished along this journey of self-discovery and deeper levels of self-acceptance and that there will be many more facets to be uncovered and polished. However, this facet of really valuing self in terms of money is crucial to discuss here as it is often a huge taboo among light workers.

In my work, blocks of abundance and money show up regularly. It shows up in undercharging by giving our time away for cheap or free. It shows up in not being able to ask for the sale. It shows up in playing small and treating your work like a hobby, not fully committing to yourself, your gifts and the world. I have seen so many healers that have invested so much in learning modality after new modality, convinced that this time they will see a return on their investment, only for nothing to change.

Of course, that was me too! Feeling guilty about charging people. Feeling like an imposter. Feeling like I still needed to know more before I could really step up and shine.

After creating all these new standards for myself, I was ready to tackle my relationship with money. I absolutely knew that my self-worth was the key! Just like my new love blueprint, I wrote out a new standard for how to value myself in business in terms of how I would receive and give to others and myself. I examined my relationship between money and time and saw so many parallels between the way I'd behaved in relationships and the way I acted around money.

I was the equivalent of a "desperado" who would stop at nothing to be loved, or in this case, pursue money. Scared to ask for love (money) as I might be rejected or seem too needy or even greedy. Yet, I was jealous of those that had more love (money) than me, thinking that love (money) was for others, but not for me. I had huge abandonment issues, please don't leave me because I might never find love (money) again and as a result, I lowered my standards to attract or keep any cheap love (money) that I could get hold of. Panic over being single and without love (money) so I would show up in my sparkliest dress to lure in love (money) but then never getting undressed to reveal what was underneath. As inauthentic as a dodgy business deal, I was too afraid that I was not good enough naked. Yes, there were still more masks to remove around external validation tied directly into my relationship with money.

I discovered that our self-worth really does reflect our net worth and that it is up to us to place that value on self. No one else gets to determine our value, we decide. That is our choice. It occurred to me that when a shopkeeper prices the products on the shelves of their store, they don't lower the price just because I might think it's too expensive. The price is the price. They know that if I don't buy it, someone else will.

Yet, so many light workers barter with their time. I know that it's because of huge hearts, yes, but it's also an invitation to explore what's underneath this resistance to charging more.

Money is created at the source, and the people it comes through are merely the channel. Knowing this has allowed me to release so much of that responsibility for the other around charging my worth. The other has the choice to decline the exchange. When we can see that it is not a personal rejection, we can be unattached to the outcome and leave our price on the shelf for the next customer to come along.

Working with my own clients in this area, one of the biggest blocks around abundance is the safety and worthiness around receiving in general. Do you know that I couldn't even enjoy a massage in the past? I would lay there feeling guilty and thinking that their thumbs were hurting. This block on receiving pleasure extended into my sex life. Always happier to be giving, deeply uncomfortable in the receiving.

We can invite abundance in by allowing ourselves to receive pleasure in these other areas. In the beginning, it can be as simple as going for that massage or employing a housecleaner. Nature shows us the way—in and out breath, tide in, tide out. If we continue to exhale without inhaling, that would not end well, and so it is with giving and receiving when it comes to our time.

Diamonds are intrinsically valuable, as are we. How do we treat them? We admire and display their beauty, we appreciate that they are rare and protect them by handling them with care, and we trust their intrinsic worth by only exchanging them for something we also deem valuable. *How about we start appreciating ourselves in this same way?*

My journey of self-worth has led me to this place. I know this is what I'm here for. Light workers are here to shine their light, to help us sparkle our brightest inner spark. Our polished inner diamonds of self-worth allow us to radiate a blinding light that ushers in this new earth. It's time. Let's release any shame around money or any stories and blocks that have kept us small. We have work to do with our light, and no part of that involves hiding.

I work with light workers who are ready to birth their sparkle into the world. I coach the strategy with a simple, step-by-step process to follow, but the most critical part is the illumination of the "inclusions" in your diamond. Both the strategy and the inner work are necessary in equal measure. Together, we can locate and deconstruct the invisible walls standing in your way so that we can take a journey to meet your self-worth. You can allow your own inner sparkle, your inner diamond to radiate your unique message without needing to know more, do more or be more.

As a next step, meet your "expanded self" in my app, which will take you through a guided visualisation to help you discover the inclusions in your self-worth diamond yet to be revealed and healed.

If I could wave my sparkly magic wand, my wish for you would be to live into the mantra, "CHOOSE YOU". With your self worth diamond polished, this inner light fully ignited, I know you will fully step into your Soul Purpose and SPARKLE!

PLAY STORE:

https://play.google.com/store/apps/details?id=com.p24073m-74hda.pklodyk5sapp

APPLE:

https://apps.apple.com/nz/app/mysparklespace/id6445849383

Jessica Reidell

Jess Reidell is an Intuitive Life and Business Coach who specializes in supporting spiritual entrepreneurs with enhancing their sales skills. She received her coaching certification from the Martha Beck Institute and has over 25 years of experience in sales, having worked as a National Franchise Sales Trainer for an International weight management company before transitioning into coaching. She lives in Dunedin Florida with her husband and mischievous American Eskimo Dog, Cinco.

The Secrets to Ageless Living

by Jessica Reidell

Greetings and welcome to the new digital Wild West. As I write this, we are approaching the summer solstice of 2023, and here in the western hemisphere we find ourselves at a fascinating point in history. The rapid spread of a massive number of new artificial intelligence support tools have just recently descended upon us. Everywhere you look it's AI this and Chat GPT that. A computer driven reality—lending credence to the preposterous notion that computers are better suited to guide humanity than humans themselves.

I call bullshit.

The "fear of missing out" or FOMO as we fondly call it these days, has me a tad curious and not wanting to be "left behind" as is the current vernacular in various memes and ads on social media. I ran across an ad recently that stated "AI will not replace humans. Humans will be replaced by humans that use AI." Again, I'm not buying it. Color me irritated as fuck. Another part of me has a visceral response when I think about jumping on the Artificial Intelligence bandwagon. It's an overall, whole body "NO" to the whole thing, particularly when it comes to creative processes such as writing, visual arts, theater and music. I find myself mourning the potential loss of leveraging genuine creativity and the unmistakable ability to truly co-create with the Divine.

I'm not trying to write a chapter raging against technology and AI tools, I promise. I do, however, want to share with certainty that no artificial intelligence tools will be used in the creation of this chapter on ageless living. This description of ageless living is a piece of my heart that I am leaving as a legacy for when I've bounced from this particular lifetime. This is a co-creation with God, Angels, Universe and whatever Spirit Guides and Guardian Angels come forth to support me in this process. This chapter is not full of suggestions about Botox or fillers or plastic surgery—oh no, no, no! Those avenues are not where true agelessness is discovered. Agelessness is an energy that we learn when we vibrate at the frequency of magic and wonder. What you are about to read is a hodge-podge of the hundreds of books I've read over the years in my search for self-improvement. They are the tenets and "life hacks" that have come my way, along with things that were taught to me by the coaches I've worked with throughout the years. Many of them are spiritual concepts that my 20 something self once poo-pooed. The same ideas that, once I revisited and experimented with them, discovered they actually worked.

Like most people, I'm fully aware that nothing of this world is truly original, and that all of the strategies I'm about to share with you below have likely been thought of or used by others who came before me. I've experimented a LOT in my life, and in doing so, by trial and error (read: PLENTY of error!") have created a way of being that has lightened my heart, softened my spirit, eased my pain and created a new found way of living that I now call "Ageless." I discovered and chose this ageless way of being by trying things on to see what worked for me and discarding what didn't.

My wish for you in reading this is that you, too, will discover and embrace a sweet, glorious and ageless way of life. Because here's the thing, your age is irrelevant. Let me say that again with a little more emphasis; YOUR AGE IS IRRELEVANT. I am here to tell you there is a better way to navigate your "wild and precious life" (Thanks, poet Mary Oliver, for coining the phrase) in this lifetime and in the ones that may follow.

As humans, we are products of social conditioning. When I was growing up, I was conditioned to believe that anyone over 50 was "old." As I write this, I am 52. As I celebrated birthdays in the decade of my 40's I began to reject the subtle cultural conditioning that dictated what was and wasn't considered appropriate for the "Mature Woman." I recall being particularly annoyed by an ad on Facebook for lipstick that was being marketed to women in their "40's, 50's and 60's" Yeah, whatever on that. Pretty broad 30-year span to put women in a box. I found these muted nudes and mauves featured in the ad to be rather boring and uninspiring. Since when do vibrant colors cease to be appealing when you hit a certain age? Says who? I felt feisty and irritated and started pushing back on the stereotypes. It was during this time that it dawned on me that this, too, was an outdated notion right up there with the expression "act your age." Act "your age?" What the hell does that even mean? When are we supposed to start "acting our age?" How about two days from NEVER. I'm not sure who authored that arbitrary, imaginary rule book but I threw it out the window a while back.

I'm going to save you some time. I'm about to share a set of perhaps "not so secret" secrets that I've adopted and put to work in my own pursuit of agelessness. I do this with the hope and the intention that you, too, can adopt and benefit from them. As you pursue an **ageless** life, you will no doubt come up with some tools and skills of your own along the way and I hope that you share the joy and pay them forward as well once you discover them. I once judged myself for my pursuit of joy, humor and pleasure as being trite and a little selfish, but along the way I realized these were the practices that took me from a life of frequent bouts of depression and dissatisfaction to one of massive abundance and joy.

Below, in no particular order, is my list.

FORGIVE YOURSELF FOR PAST MISTAKES.

This is a critical step in aging backwards. There is no Botox for a wrinkled soul. If your baggage is heavy, you can always give yourself relief by setting it down. Walking through life riddled with guilt will make you feel old and sad and heavy. Giving yourself grace through small acts of forgiveness will unburden your spirit and lighten your soul. Here's an example. I once blew an audition for a part I really wanted in a play. I auditioned in Seattle for the female lead of Maggie in Tennessee Williams' "Cat on a Hot Tin Roof" Both the director and the stage manager complimented my cold reading and I got a callback shortly after the audition. I was fresh out of a failed marriage at the time and I wasn't taking particularly good care of myself. I was partying hard, keeping bad company, staying up too late. Long story short I completely blew the callback, arriving after the callback time and doing a less than stellar second reading. I remember seeing the look of disappointment on the stage manager's face when we locked eyes. Who knows if I would have gotten the part, but I most certainly would have had a better shot by showing up on time and being at my best. I actually blew a few more auditions in a similar fashion before I wised up and acknowledged the fact that I was getting in my own way. I realized after avoiding theater auditions for many more years than I'd like to admit that I was carrying some heavy weight of shame and guilt about that specific incident and others. I made a list of this and other things that were weighing me down, and made a ritual by burning the list. This felt so freeing. Forgiveness is key. What do you need to forgive yourself for in order to move forward? Write these things down, acknowledge them, forgive yourself and have compassion for the person you were when you did these things and then **LET THEM GO**. By doing this, you will set yourself free to be back on a path of joy. Having past events you feel guilty about won't keep you from an ageless life, but beating yourself up about them will. Release them and step into a new way of being that truly serves you on your path forward.

ACKNOWLEDGE AND APPRECIATE THE THINGS YOU LOVE TO DO, AND THE THINGS YOU TRULY LOVE ABOUT YOURSELF.

Are you in touch with these things? Like, truly in touch with them? There is so much joy to be had in re-discovering the things that light you up when you do them, and the way you light up the world with the qualities and energy that are unique to you that you bring to the world. Things you appreciate about yourself that may or may not be appreciated by others. It does not matter. You do not need another individual to validate the reality of any of your good qualities. Make a list of the top 10 things you love to do, and re-incorporate what may have fallen out of your life. Your inner child will thank you. Now make a list of the top 10 things you love and appreciate most about YOURSELF. Reflect on this list and add to it often, especially as you continue to evolve. Once we learn to have a heartfelt and genuine appreciation of ourselves and the way we show up in the world, the need for outside approval begins to dissolve and eventually disappear. Like magic. Try it. It might feel weird at first but eventually you'll get the hang of it. Pinky swear.

BE GRATEFUL FOR ALL THAT YOU HAVE AND ALL THAT YOU DESIRE THAT ISN'T HERE YET.

There was a time I used to roll my eyes when other people spoke of the importance of gratitude and being grateful. Now I know that a master accelerator for manifestation comes through a grateful heart. Gratitude opens up a portal which allows more good to flow towards you. We won't get what we desire if we continue to focus on lack or what it is we are yearning for that we do not yet have. Quoting Abraham-Hicks here: "Focus on what you WANT, NOT what you DON'T want." At 46 years old when I finally put this into practice instead of acting like a master skeptic when it came to spiritual principles it was as if a dam broke and the things I desired or wanted to happen began to flow in my direction as if by magic.

If you are finding it hard to be grateful for the things you actually have in your life right now, try this exercise. Imagine that everything you currently own was stripped away from you. The people in your life. All of your money. Your car, your home, your clothing, your belongings. Imagine lying cold, naked and alone on the sidewalk, wondering how in the fresh hell you wound up here.

Who would you be with nothing? Sit with this feeling for at least 10-15 minutes. Make a plan as to how to move forward. Then, imagine a genie appears and gives you just one wish, and you wish to get back everything precious in your life that you just lost and it all reappears.

You'll have instantaneous mad gratitude for all that was returned and all that you have—**RIGHT NOW**.

JUST LAUGH. MAKE AN EFFORT TO FIND THE HUMOR IN EVERYTHING IN YOUR DAY-TO-DAY LIFE.

There's nothing quite like humor. Witty banter, puns and plays on words go a long way towards keeping things light, fun and **ageless**. Humor is not limited to jokes, although it's always a good thing to have a few good jokes in your back pocket. If you're single, find a person who you can laugh with. If you're married or in a relationship, find more reasons to laugh with your partner. Laugh at yourself when you can. Laugh at it all. Life is absolutely too short not to crack up as much as you possibly can. I once found great humor during a road trip when I broke a crown biting into an onion ring from Burger King. There was a rock in it or some shit that was hard and cracked my fake tooth. I was already back on the road and decided not to go back there and show them the rock and make an issue out of it. I laughed instead that it might have been funny to do so. Going back to Burger *KING* to get the *CROWN*. Heh, heh. Get it?

ACT AS IF EVERYONE IS HITTING ON YOU.

This is one of my absolute favorites. It came to be when I was going through my divorce in my late 20's. I craved connection and physical touch, so I would give hand massages at parties and use the time to connect with my friends, most of whom were actors. Once whilst massaging a friend's hand, a catty woman approached me and stated in a smarmy tone; "You know when you do that, Jess, everyone thinks you are hitting on them." I paused for a second, ss the brilliance of turning this statement around hit me. "Well, what I like to do…" I said thoughtfully, "Is to assume **EVERYONE** is **AL-WAYS** hitting on me. That way I have a much better time."

This stuck with me for decades. I still do it! Most of my close friends are in on this little secret of mine. It's an energy tool, a trick that really works. Don't believe me? Try a few scenarios:

Walk into a social situation with a case of nerves. Wonder if anyone will like you or talk to you or even acknowledge you exist. Act like a wallflower. Read the room. See what happens.

On another day try a different social scenario. Walk in like you own the place. Assume everyone is hitting on you and wants to connect with you and vibe in your aura. They all want you! Feel the difference as to how people respond to you in both scenarios. Decide which one you prefer. Rinse and repeat. (Credit to Martha Beck for educating me further on how one's energy and vibration impacts a roomful of people.)

LIVE IN THE MOMENT.

This is something I make a point to teach my clients. When we are mired down with **FEAR** or **WORRY**, we are in the future. When we are in a sea of anger or regret, we are in the past. This steals our joy and does not allow us to be fully present for the beautiful moments that make up our lives. It's easy to get caught up in rushing from one task to the next, or spending way too much time thinking about something bad that happened before or something you are worried about that may never actually happen! Relinquish the need to dwell on the future or the past. Writer and Spiritual Teacher Wayne Dyer classifies guilt and worry as "useless emotions" At first this did not make complete sense to me; however, I came to understand how dwelling in these energies serves the good of no one. My husband and I go boating every Sunday, weather permitting. Our boat log says "Be here now" on the cover. Sage advice. Also, another tip: being on a boat has a way of keeping you in the present moment. Something else to try!

WALK THROUGH YOUR LIFE WITH A GENUINE SENSE OF WONDER AND ENCHANTMENT!

This ties in with being present. If you are not present, you won't notice the spellbinding moments that are happening right **NOW**. At **NOW** O'Clock and not a second later. We of the "woo" have learned how to do this. Live your life with a sense of wonder and enchantment. Each day, appreciate the magic of both the simple and the complex and watch your appreciation for the little things soar! I know this may sound like corny "stop and smell the roses" kinda stuff, but give it a shot before you knock it for being cheesy. This practice keeps you present and enhances your life in a way you can't possibly understand until you do it and keep living it.

LET WHOEVER THINK WHATEVER THEY WANT.

There's a meme that is circulating on social media right now that after the age of 40 the only weight you should worry about losing is the weight of other people's opinions. This couldn't be more true. The 21st century version of Henry David Thoreau's quote "The mass of men lead lives of quiet desperation" would likely be "Most people make choices and live their lives to please others rather than themselves." Are you still tied up caring about what other people think?

Even if you think you're not doing it, I assure you that on a subconscious level, you are.

We've been conditioned for **YEARS** to "fit in."

"Run with the pack."

"Fall in line."

"**CONFORM** to the **NORM**."

It goes back for generations. We needed our tribes and communities in order to survive. One false move and you could be kicked out, banished from your group and wind up starving, cold, naked and alone. When I began to rediscover some of my mystical gifts, at first, I felt an unexplainable terror. I was afraid people would think I was "crazy."

Many did. And yet here I am. Still standing.

It takes time to recondition your nervous system to know that you can blaze your own trail and go against the grain. **KNOW THIS,** "Your uniqueness is what makes you magic."

Dr. Seuss says:

> *"Why fit in when you were born to stand out?"*

(This is one of my favorites now)

Here's a fun activity. Make a list of the ways in which you are still stifling your self-expression. Who are you trying to please? What's the worst thing that could happen if you say what you think and march to the beat of a different drummer? (I'll give you a hint: you'll unload some people who are not aligned to be in your life and you'll be grateful you did!)

You **DESERVE** to be **YOU. ALL** of **YOU.** Your magical, authentic self.

The more you step into this, the more **AGELESS** you become. So, own your weird. **LET WHOEVER THINK WHATEVER.** If they don't like the real you, then encourage them to beat a path out of your stratosphere. Like, stat.

SLEEP.

Okay, I know this might seem a little obvious but hear me out. Back in my 30's, there was something I used to say to myself when I was having a rough day, was feeling low energy or felt overwhelmed with a decision I was wrestling with: "A good night's sleep fixes **EVERYTHING**." When things were off balance or life itself was making my head spin like Beelzebub, I knew a good night's sleep would help me see things with new eyes the following day. Shitty day? Struggling with a decision? Put yourself to bed an hour or two earlier and make sure to clock however many hours you need to feel like a new person. Other great by products of getting a little extra sleep that I noticed was an easier time shedding a few unwanted pounds and clearer skin, along with a much clearer mind!

HAVE FRIENDS OF ALL AGES!

You've heard that age is only a number, and it is. To be truly ageless and be high functioning and empathetic to others in society. it's super valuable to have friends of many different ages—both younger and older than you. I do aquafit with people in their sixties and seventies. One of my best friends is in her 30's, eighteen years younger than me. I love her to pieces. I network and socialize with lots of people in their 20's. With friends of all ages, you get exposed to many dynamics and perspectives that you would not otherwise comprehend. You are able to see what is going on with different generations, and how that may be different from yours. In doing this, you get a better understanding of where different people are coming from. And that keeps you connected, and dialed in, and feeling young and **HAPPY**! I am so grateful to my Millennial friends for explaining all the generational idiosyncrasies that I don't fully understand as a Gen Xer. And seeing that understanding the language that Gen Z is using practically requires a translator so I am thrilled that my stepson is part of that generation! I look to my friends in their sixties and seventies for their wisdom, life experience and politically incorrect humor. I look to my friends in their 30's and 40's when I have technical questions, need a different brand of humor and when I want to stay current on what's "in" and what's "out." I say all of this to say, if you are only fraternizing with people in your own age group, consider making some new friends. Strike up conversations with people 10-15 years younger and 10-15 years older than you. Get to know them as people. Learn what they value most, what they enjoy doing and what they need support with. Get outside of your comfort zone and get connected with people of many different ages. You'll get new perspectives from many folks you may have not otherwise connected with. This will truly assist you in your journey to live agelessly.

LOVE AND CHERISH YOUR PARTNER IN LIFE IF YOU HAVE ONE.

People often ask my husband and I how we stay so happily married. It's actually a few pretty simple tricks that I'm delighted to share in list form below:

1. **CHOOSE** each other every day. Every day is a new day to acknowledge your decision and commitment to be with your partner or spouse.

2. Don't ever take your partner for granted. You get a new chance to love and respect your partner every day and to be loved and respected by your partner. This privilege is earned by both parties daily.

3. Find out what's important to the other person and do more of that. Read the *Five Languages of Love* by Gary Chapman. Do the Love Languages quiz with your partner or spouse; you'll learn so much. Learn to speak their love language.

4. Reconsider trying to change your partner. People change when they want to, not when you want them to.

5. Communicate effectively. Seriously. No one can read your mind nor should they have to try to do so.

6. Don't be clingy or codependent. Big turnoff. Be an adult.

7. Threatening to leave the relationship during petty arguments is ill-advised. You'll wind up looking like "The Boy who cried Wolf" and it's not a good look.

8. Establish the boundaries and deal breakers in the relationship and don't cross those lines.

9. Acknowledge the things you appreciate about your partner. Share them.

10. Make time for sex. The longer you go without connecting in an intimate way, the more distant you become from your partner. Stay committed to a schedule of regular sexual activity that works for both parties.

11. Say "I love you" often. You'll be glad you did.

Lately in my world, I've been witnessing a few couples I love and have known for years splitting up. It's been rather heartbreaking. I've been thinking a lot lately about what the actual catalysts are for break-ups that happen many years into a relationship. Like, what straw was really the one that broke the camel's back? I gave up on overthinking this, as I realized that the reasons are likely far too nuanced for me to fully understand. We never truly know what's going on between people and besides, it's really none of our business. In light of this recent phenomenon, I said to my husband when we were out on the boat recently "Whatever issues arise at this stage of our marriage I hope that we are able to work through it. It's not that I couldn't go it alone, I just don't want to." He took my hand in that moment and kissed it and said "Neither do I." I got a little teary then and I get a little teary now just thinking about it. Staying committed takes a strong intention, and both parties must be committed to staying in the relationship.

PUT GOOD, WHOLESOME WHOLE FOODS IN YOUR BODY.

I recommend using the 80-20 rule on this one. Let 80% of what you consume be whole foods. Vegetables, fruits, lean protein, heart healthy fats. Consume starches and refined sugars in moderation. I used to be on the "low fat" bandwagon but the chemicals in some of those products outweigh the benefits of consuming less fat. The fact that the food industry convinced us that margarine was supposedly "healthier" than butter has me shaking my head in disgust to this day. If you look at photos of people on the beach in the1970's, they were slim and fit looking. Today so many are obese and unhealthy. Watch for new pseudonyms for GMOs too. The language on food labels keep changing. I'm also a fan of some specific supplements that have given me tremendous benefits, and lately my husband and I have been feeling vibrant and energized with a daily dose of powdered greens. Find what makes your body feel good. Back when I listened to Tony Robbins collection of cassette tapes on Personal Power, something he said always stuck with me. Before you eat something, ask yourself the question; "Will this **CLEANSE** me, or **CLOG** me?" It's a great way to make better choices when it comes to your food intake. When I worked in the weight management industry, I often heard excuses like "I don't have time to eat healthy." Well, it takes about the same amount of time to eat an apple as it does a Big Mac, so there goes that excuse.

DON'T LIE. TO ANYONE, ESPECIALLY NOT YOURSELF.

My life took a dramatic swing in the right direction when I realized I was rationalizing things to the degree that I was literally lying to *myself*. Once I realized in my late 20's that lying to myself was the ultimate form of self-deception and delusion, my life was enhanced exponentially. Lying is a character flaw. Don't do it. You dig a hole that you have to keep on digging. I'm not saying run around insulting people in the name of truth telling; be discerning and be kind, but don't spin tales that are not true.

IF YOU ARE UNHAPPY ABOUT SOMETHING, CHANGE IT.

Life is too short to hang out in places and spaces that make you miserable. Happiness is a choice. So is unhappiness. If you hate your job and it's contributing to misery instead of mirth, then by all means GTFO. The same goes for bad marriages and lousy partnerships. Also, friendships. If someone is no longer supporting your goals, or is unpleasant to be around, or brings no value to your life, it's time to make a change. Look out for number 1 and you can't go wrong.

CREATE A LIFE MOTTO THAT KEEPS YOU CONNECTED TO WHAT BRINGS YOU JOY.

My motto in life is "to always have a great time no matter what." I made this particular wish when I was 22 at Mardi Gras in New Orleans and I threw a coin in a fountain. It stuck with me. I went on to make that same wish every time I tossed another coin in a fountain, and I still do it when I blow out birthday candles or catch sight of a shooting star. When I find myself in a situation where I'm not having a good time, I make a hasty exit or find a way to lighten my mood or make things more fun. Having a life motto is great. Get one if you don't have one! It's worked out pretty damn well for me and my ageless self.

STAY GROUNDED IN YOUR COMMITMENT TO BEING AN AGELESS SOUL.

As Wayne Dyer shared, "You are not a human being having a spiritual experience, you are a spiritual being having a human experience." This is also challenging to wrap your mind around at first. It's imperative, however, that you comprehend this as you deepen your commitment to living an ageless life. Remind yourself often that you can access the state of being limitless and that your soul and your energy are **AGELESS**.

When I moved to Florida, I got a vanity license plate that says AGELES J (The word "Ageless" was already taken, go figure) The plate is a great and constant reminder of the energy of the way I choose to be. I also have a few good friends that always point me back to my chosen ageless path whenever doubt creeps in.

Living an ageless life is only one decision away. We don't need to stop basking in childlike wonder simply because of the number of years we've logged on the planet. This is mere social conditioning, which has given so many people a bum steer to an incredibly bleak and uninspiring outlook on life. Grab hold and embrace the things that make you feel the most vibrant and alive. The things that make **YOU** the most "**YOU**" that you can be. Then rinse and repeat. It really is that simple.

This is just a small sampling of the tools and ideas that I help my clients use to connect with their essential selves and live authentically and agelessly. I hope you are leaving with a newfound appreciation for what it means to ground into a life of wonder, joy, gratitude, love and ageless energy. My wish for you is that one or more of the ideas I've shared in this chapter have landed with you and had a profound impact. The ideas themselves are just the beginning, it's the implementation and repetition of them that will truly enhance the quality of your life.

If you would like to speak with me further about working on your own ageless life design or have questions about my two signature coaching programs "Ageless" or "Move Your Magic Meter" please go to my website agelessjess.com to book a call. I also currently support spiritual entrepreneurs with enhancing their sales skills to maximize their revenue, so if you have a spiritual coaching business and need support, please reach out to connect.

Jess Reidell, Sales Success Coach
jess@jessreidellcoaching.com; cell: 404-543-7767

Please book a free consultation with me at:

https://calendly.com/jess-33/20

Nan Leffingwell

As a Mindfulness Teacher and Certified Online Breathwork Facilitator with more than 300 hours of training under her belt, Nan Leffingwell is passionate about teaching the way to peace and presence. At Tymbal Mindfulness Coaching, her eclectic teacher's toolbox empowers clients to create more peace in their lives, pairing formal meditation with presence-building life activities.

Limit Less

by Nan Leffingwell

What prevents a person from living the life they desire? Ninety-nine percent of all humans on earth are not born into a royal family, with a high IQ, access to an Ivy League education, or with two parents who have the time and energy to nurture every part of their lives. Millions of people's achievements would not have been feasible if those were the only conditions for living a meaningful and rewarding life. How do people like Walt Disney, born into a humble family with just a high school education, go on to build Walt Disney Animation Studios? It wasn't about how hard he worked in school or that he was a good student, which he wasn't. Instead, it was about how he spent his time after school. Each day Walt got up early to deliver newspapers, and with the extra money, he took a correspondence course in cartooning, which he studied and practiced after school. Walt delivered papers all through high school, then worked as an ambulance driver, and continued to invest his spare time and money in developing his art skills. While he may have come from a simple background, he did not allow his circumstances to limit his beliefs about what was possible. I am sure fear showed up for him about his future; Walt Disney was human after all, and he pursued his dream to have a creative career during the Great Depression. While people stood in soup lines, Walt worked hard to become really good at cartooning. And what he also got really good at was not allowing fear to distract him from his dream. As the nation began to recover from the crushing poverty of the Depression, it was the work of Walt Disney that ushered in the "Golden Age of Animation," which entertained and lifted people's spirits. A limiting belief can be one of the most powerful barriers that keep people from living the life they dream of.

A limiting belief is the internal dialogue of our thoughts that tend toward the negative, kind of like a backseat driver that describes a gory car accident rather than help find safer routes. Limiting beliefs are the programming in the background that cause us to do things like pick the wrong career or partner. Limiting beliefs can be hard to change, especially if a person is unaware that they exist deep in subconscious thought and feeling patterns. What if I told you there is a practice that requires just 12 minutes of your time each day that, when practiced consistently over time, helps one become aware of their hidden limiting beliefs, empowers them to change their thoughts and feelings, and opens them up to their true potential? Would you think it involves a complex ritual invoking entities existing in other dimensions, or maybe it is an expensive pill with mysterious ingredients from the primeval timbers of Scandinavia? It is none of those things; instead, it is the practice of mindfulness meditation. The simple act of turning off the TV and putting down the phone to sit for just 12 minutes a day and focus the mind is one of the most powerful tools there is to unlock unlimited potential.

Before I go into what mindfulness is, we need to clear something up that online viral marketing has confused: mindfulness is not just a hashtag used on pretty photos selling crystals on Instagram. Mindfulness is not an aesthetic; it is a practice, a discipline, and a way of being. Mindfulness meditation uses several mediation techniques that help develop the skill of being more aware in each moment of the day. Sounds so easy, right? Too good to be true? Unfortunately, in our materialist society filled with distractions, meditation can be one of the hardest habits to start and keep.

The vast majority of us rush through our busy work days, reacting to one problem after another, only to come home exhausted after work. Once we are at home doing chores like making dinner, we continue to think about that problem at work or worry about how to pay an extra bill. Then after dinner, we plop down somewhere comfy and stare at a screen, escaping into a story or social media. That escape may seem to feel better in the moment, but when the next day comes and we do that same pattern of work, worry, and escape all over again, we wonder why the things we want for our lives are not appearing. We have all been stuck at some point. Some of us have escaped this cycle, and some of us haven't yet. I escaped, and just so you know, I am not writing this from a remote beach resort where I have fresh fruit delivered each morning for breakfast. I get up and put in eight or more hours Monday through Friday, just like everyone else. But how I do it, what gets done, and how I experience it are so much more fulfilling now. Because I do it with self-awareness and a growing sense of gratitude for this precious gift of life each and every day. I am living my dream life working like everyone else, with a mortgage, credit card debt, and weeds in the garden. But also, with a purpose I am so passionate about, I look forward to waking up each morning and feel blessed to be able to pursue it.

Here is a little bit about me and how I transformed my life. What I described before about the daily grind and repeating the same day over and over again is exactly how I spent 20 years trying to build a career, chasing the reward carrot dangled out in front of me at the end of the performance review stick. And then I stopped. I stepped out of that game in 2017 after losing both of my parents within a six-month period. They were hardworking, good parents who made sure that their kids had their survival and education needs met. And about the time my dad was preparing to retire, he suffered from a debilitating spinal disease that slowly got progressively worse until he could no longer move. After 20 years of pain and dementia, he was gone. There were no golden years he had worked so hard to save for, only medical bills and pain. I suddenly found myself grieving the loss of my parents and wondering, "What is this grind of a life for?" I was grieving and completely lost when I decided to step off the career ladder and heal before my time on this planet ran out. I did not know what to do specifically, other than decide to stop doing what it was that I was doing because clearly, it was not working.

Even though I did okay financially at the software company, what was not working was the damage I was doing to my body. I managed two teams, one of which ran 24 hours a day, seven days a week. Stuck on the mid-level manager rung of the career ladder, I was tipping the scale past 300 pounds, having near daily migraines, pounding aspirin and acetaminophen, drinking copious amounts of coffee, and eating fast food to keep getting work done in a busy schedule. I was exhausted from trying to prove myself to the corporate overlords, and now, after losing my parents and grieving, I quit. I decided to go out on my own and work as an independent contractor for other software companies.

After launching my business with just one client and not having to answer to anyone else's eight-to-five schedule, I made the time to go to the gym, quit sugar, and meet new people. Because I was attending a lot of small business and personal improvement kind of events, the new people I was getting to know were small entrepreneurs that were in the wellness industry of some sort: yoga teachers, therapists, and breathworkers. These new people introduced me to many new practices and techniques for self-improvement. Over the next four years with dedicated practice to learning new ways of being and thinking, I become a certified breathwork facilitator, trained as a mindfulness meditation teacher, and now I am a completely different person. I am more than 100 pounds lighter, with energy that actually lasts throughout the entire day. I sleep well, and I maybe get a headache once every two months. The peace and gratitude I feel for this existence is so much deeper and wider than ever before. I have totally transformed my life, and now I help other people transform theirs. But don't be fooled, for my transformation was not a gradual line of improvement that always charted upwards. It was full of moments of self-sabotage, struggle, and the discovery of deeper levels of work that needed to be done. There is one thing that the ego is really good at, and that is keeping people exactly as they are. Breaking lifelong ways of being is really hard work. The journey from where I was to where I am now is too complex for this small chapter. I want you to have enough information from an example of how limiting beliefs can be transformed so that you can get started right away with meditation. I am not going to fill this chapter with another mind-numbing history of the development of meditation methods, quotes from great teachers, or copious amounts of data about neuroscience. Instead, I am going to tell you a story about one of my old limiting beliefs and how I transformed it. And with this one small example, I hope to give you enough information to get started right away on transforming one of your own limiting beliefs.

I struggle with a limiting belief and fear that first appeared around public speaking and self-promotion. It started after I launched my mindfulness business and realized I needed to do more work on sales. For my technology business, I get new clients through referrals, and while I love to work with people to help them learn technology and feel confident using it, I prefer to teach about mindfulness meditation as it is a practice that can help people learn anything, not just technology. You see, when I start to work with any new technology client, the topic that begins every single conversation is the client's fear of technology. They are afraid they may lose files or that it will be too difficult or expensive, and they always fear doing something wrong. As a technology teacher, I gently guide them through enough processes with just the right amount of encouragement to indirectly and slowly address the real problem, which isn't technology; it is never about technology; the real problem is the fear and story that are built up around it. When I teach about mindfulness mediation, I have the freedom to go straight to whatever issue is creating a problem in a person's life and hand them a tool that gets them started transforming it immediately. I love to see people learn how to become self-empowered to make the changes they want in their lives and take off on their new journey of self-discovery and finding life's potential. My mindfulness business allows me to experience more diverse teaching and learn from other people because every human life is so unique and diverse.

Wanting to take my mindfulness business from random conversations with local like-minded people to many new people on the internet, I knew that one of the skills I would need to understand and improve was sales. I knew that ignoring sales like it didn't exist was not going to help if I wanted to get my message out to new and different people. So, I signed up for a course that provided that training and met some great salespeople. This course also provided the opportunity to speak to a group of nearly 800 people who were interested in all sorts of personal development topics at a three-day online event. The writing of the talk was easy. But when I was practicing my talk with friends, the thought of being in front of 800 strangers caused fear to suddenly appear out of nowhere. I did drama club in high school, performed in plays, and I love talking to people, but for some reason, after all these years, being seen and heard by so many people made my ego show up and shout "Danger!" I developed an old-fashioned case of stage fright. There it was—fear, and its source was a limiting belief about being judged. I know intellectually that while some people may be negative, there will also be people out there who want to hear my message and be positive. I know that it is impossible to please everyone all of the time, and I dropped my people-pleasing tendency a long time ago. But this limiting belief had enough power to charge up a sense of fear in my subconscious. I knew I was going to need to disconnect this feeling of fear from public speaking and reconnect public speaking to a new feeling. And the way that I did that was with mindfulness meditation and relying on the innate human resource of neuroplasticity.

One of the mindfulness meditation techniques that is a part of "mindfulness-based stress reduction," or MBSR for short, is called the body-scan meditation, and in this practice, the meditator focuses all the mind's attention on the body and how the body feels. In a guided body scan mediation, the facilitator will often guide the meditator from head to toe with verbal prompts to pay attention to things like if the surface of the skin feels hot or cold or if there is tightness in a muscle. This practice helps the meditator get out of their thoughts and become more aware of their bodies. We often overlook our body as a source of knowledge or wisdom, but more and more research is coming out about how important the body is to self-awareness.

I wanted to find the source of this fear in my body, so I began to do body scan meditations daily to observe how specific feelings would show up in my body as I thought about public speaking. I immediately discovered two big sensations that would occur in my body every time. As I would bring my attention to my neck, I could feel a heavy burning knot right at the base of my throat. And when I would bring my attention to my back, I could feel every muscle get tight to the point that it was almost like my spine locked into place and I could not move. I decided to work with each of these two sensations by sitting quietly in meditation and allowing myself to feel the uncomfortable emotions that came up. I knew that somewhere in the past, each of those physical feelings must have had an emotion attached to them from an experience.

As the event began to approach, I took the time to meditate on allowing my mind to stay with the physical sensations that kept coming up when I thought about public speaking. I started with the knot in my throat and focused on remembering a time when I had felt that before, and then it dawned on me that I had experienced stage fright before, many years before, and the memory came flooding back. It happened when I was 11, and my father and mother were being honored with a big party for charity that they had worked very hard to raise money for. The party was in a ballroom at a fancy hotel. I can remember to this day how the ballroom sparkled with huge crystal chandeliers, gold-trimmed wallpaper, and every table had a huge flower centerpiece with glowing candles. There was a live band that played music from the big band era. All the women were in long, flowing kaftan dresses that sparkled with sequins and gold embroidery. I was in awe of the beauty that had been brought together in one room to create such a magical ambiance. It was the type of thing I had only ever seen in old movies. Shortly before the event, the organizers thought it would be nice for us kids to say something to our parents as a part of the presentation. I was chosen to deliver a few sentences with my two brothers standing on either side. The assignment seemed easy enough, but once I walked out on that stage, saw the venue and the hundreds of people with all their eyes on me and my brothers, an overwhelming fear took hold of me. We walked up on stage to the microphone, and it was my turn to speak. But I couldn't speak. There I stood, feeling barely able to breathe, let alone speak. I felt helpless, unable to say what I so desperately wanted to say to my parents. One of my brothers put his hand on my back to support and encourage me. I looked up at him, and he nodded with his eyes, saying to me, "Go ahead, you can do it." I could feel his encouragement, and I looked at my other brother at my side, and he whispered, "You can do it, Nancy," and he even mouthed the words I was to speak. So, I looked out at the crowd and moved my lips, but barely any air could pass through my vocal cords. Fortunately, my older brother came to my rescue and leaned down and spoke the words louder for everyone to hear into the microphone. Everyone thought that was pretty adorable anyway, and I was relieved.

That first memory of stage fright was one piece of the puzzle. But there was another piece that kept me frozen in place. That feeling of my spine being so tight I was unable to move had a source, and as I allowed myself to feel into that in the next day's meditation, another memory about a time of fear appeared. That memory took place in a location completely opposite of the ballroom; it was in the timber behind our house in the country. The timber surrounded the house on two sides and gave the house a natural privacy. For us kids, it was the most amazing playground that we had all to ourselves for our adventures and discoveries. The timber was a deep and thick wood that created the most beautiful canvas of color that changed with every season. In the deep center of the wood was a sandy-bottom creek that zigzagged its way through the middle. With it being so shallow, each winter it would freeze solid, and we would "skate" on the surface in our stocking feet. Along the banks of the frozen creek, we would see the openings of burrows for meadow mice, muskrats, and groundhogs, sleeping peacefully in the quiet timber. In the spring, the timber came alive with the trees budding, animals coming out of hibernation, and growing tinder shoots of wild asparagus and morel mushrooms. In the summer, the canopy was so dense that the woods were dark and cool, protecting us from the heat. In the fall, the colorful garden spiders made their giant webs across the paths. But the timber's glory was mid-summer, with every limb covered in leaves still drinking in the spring rains and charging with the sunlight from a Kansas kettle blue sky. Every color of green was present, from yellow to deep green blue, on a canvas filled with trees of all kinds.

Dad would take us on walks into the timber to find rocks polished in the creek, and he would teach us how to identify trees by their bark, birds by their song, and animals by their tracks. The years of leaf fall in this thick wood created the perfect biome for morel mushrooms that we would hunt in the spring. Coming home with a bag of morels made us heroes at dinner time. We would clean the morels in salt water so the bugs would come out of the nooks and crannies, and then we would dredge them in egg wash and crushed crackers that mom would fry to golden perfection. Before each expedition to find these precious mushrooms, dad would guide us to look very closely before reaching down and plucking the treasure of the morel too fast. We needed to be on the lookout for timber rattlers, which are the exact same color as the dead leaves the morels grew in. We would gear up for a trip to the timber with our thick cowboy boots and heavy jeans. And we would each grab a long garden tool like a weeding hoe. With tool in hand dad would remind us on how to use it if we saw a snake. If the snake was about 12 feet away, run. If it was six feet away, freeze and watch. And if it was up close within striking distance, we were to put the business end of the weeding hoe between the snake's fangs and our ankles.

On a late summer day, our family friend Toby came to play. With my brothers and me, the four of us headed down to the creek. Our plan was to play in the cool creek, so we did not have on our boots or jeans; we were wearing shorts and our cloth sneakers; mine were a pair of hand-me-down white converse that I loved. We had a devoted and loyal German shepherd who was always making sure to protect us kids. Duchess was a beautiful and intelligent dog who knew at all times where we kids were. She watched over us like a devoted and loyal mother. As we headed into the timber Duchess ran ahead to check the path in front of us and then would run back to ensure that we were all sticking together and headed in the same direction. Back and forth she went, the process of scouting forward and returning to verify the way was safe. We got into the cover of the timber and started the climb down to the low cement bridge. There we were along the muddy banks at the cement bridge, excited to discover skinks, snails, butterflies, and animal tracks. We started to spread out on the cement bridge. With me being the slowest of the group with my short legs, I hadn't quite reached the edge of the cement bridge yet. Duchess seemed to be cautiously inspecting something on the other side. Brett, Toby, Shawn, and I were each several feet apart when Duchess began a low growl, pointing at the tall grass on the other side of the cement bridge. We all began walking in her direction as she began barking louder and fiercer. Toby was the closest, and as he leaned over the tall grass, he yelled, "Snakes! **LOTS OF SNAKES**!" There was a large colony of snakes all gathered together, sunning themselves, and at that moment Duchess lunged toward the pile snapping and barking. From their sunning bed, the snakes shot out fast headed toward the creek, but we were standing between them and the safety of the water. Brett yelled, "Run, Nancy!" I was frozen in place, unable to move my feet. It felt like a metal rod was holding me in place, from my head to the soles of my feet. I watched as what seemed like hundreds of snakes continuously shot out from their bed and slithered over our shoes and around our ankles. They were moving so fast, and the boys danced in place, lifting one foot after another, trying to move their feet away from the snakes, and as soon as it had begun, it was over. They disappeared beneath the water. In dead silence we watched the surface of the water settle. I can't remember now who it was that said, "Is anyone bit?" and relief washed over me as the other two boys said, "Not me." And then they all turned and looked at me, still frozen in place, unblinking, and unable to move. Brett walked up, put his hand on my shoulder, checked my ankles, and said, "It's okay, we just spooked them; they were more afraid of us." We decided not to wade and play in the creek that day. Instead, we ran back to the house, excited to be the first to tell the tale of our adventure to dad. Dad suspected we had stirred up a colony of diamond-backed water snakes, which fortunately for us are completely harmless.

Intellectually, I know that being judged and a bed of potentially poisonous snakes do not deserve the same level of fear. Neural patterns get formed for a lot of reasons, and while I wonder why stage fright suddenly appeared, what is more important is that we humans have the power to create new and more empowering neural patterns through a type of "rewiring" process. I knew that what I needed to do was connect public speaking to different feelings, and memories could be a source of fuel for generating new feelings. I needed to create a feeling of safety and inspiration and then connect those feelings to public speaking.

While the timber was a place of snakes, it was also a place of great refuge for me as a child. I loved the solitude of the timber. I loved learning the songs of birds and getting them to reply to my whistles. I loved how the timber changed color with the seasons. There was a meadow that I loved so much, filled with native grasses and flowers. When the milkweed bloomed, I loved to sit and watch the fat bumble bees and flurry of butterflies. There was an old tree that looked like a deer dipping its head down to drink from the creek. The cement bridge, the meadow of wild flowers, and the path covered by the shade of trees was a tranquil space. Being in the country with very few people around, I was encouraged to roam freely and play, with the only rule being to be home by sunset and use my skills taught by dad to stay safe. I loved my existence as a wandering hermit, gardening, yard work, and communing with the birds and bugs. Not many people on earth have the blessing of a childhood like I did, and as I get older, my gratitude for it gets deeper and deeper. I would use the good memories of the timber as a place of refuge and peace to remind myself of the serenity and safety that I have now in my home and office.

Now I needed another feeling to counter the feeling of being judged. After a couple days of spending time with my memories, I had another memory that I could use for inspiration. My mother had a beautiful singing voice—truly beautiful. We lived in a small town, and mom became known for her singing at funerals. I remember many a Saturday afternoon where I would attend a funeral with mom where she had been requested to sing. I was often brought along, all dressed up and given clear instructions not to bother anyone, and would sit in the back of the funeral parlor while mom lifted the hearts of the hurting with Ave Maria or How Great Thou Art. I could see the relief people felt when the music allowed the grief to express itself. The crying got a bit louder, and people would lean into the shoulders of family members who held and consoled them. Even though I often did not know the person whose funeral it was, I got a sense of the person from the feeling in that room when the music began. I remember how grateful people were to mom for the love her voice expressed for their departed.

In the few days just before my speaking event, I intentionally visualized and felt my office as my sanctuary and refuge to create a feeling of safety and felt the feeling of helping someone with my voice like my mom would with her singing. This is what I would aspire to, and whether a person understood my entire presentation or just one sentence, with the clear intention in my mind and the compassionate feeling in my heart. The fear melted away. On the day of the event, I was able to present, it was well received, and I had several people reached out to ask about my training. I am so grateful that I did not allow that fear keep me from connecting with people and sharing what it is to have a human experience.

There is so much more to the nuance of mindfulness meditation and neuroscience, but in this short chapter I have summarized the secret formula for change: become aware that a limiting belief exists, explore what feelings are attached to that belief, and attach a new feeling to start a new behavior. Our thoughts become feelings, feelings become behaviors, and behaviors become a life. Once you become a student of your mind, body, and experience, you not only learn how you got to where you are but also how to plot a course for where you want to go.

I hope that in my story you found something that could be helpful to you in your journey. And if you would like to learn more about how mindfulness meditation can support you and your well-being, take a look at my website, found at **tymbalmindfulness.com**, for the resources available there. If you would like to talk to me about a personalized approach in starting the practice of mindfulness meditation, go to **chatwithnan.com**. I would love to have a no-pressure chat where we discuss what it is you would like to transform and if mindfulness meditation is right for you. Thank you for taking the time to read the story of one example of transformation. And just like I end all my meditations, it is my profound wish for you that you are well, that you are safe, and that you are happy.

Luis Melendez Jr.

With his diverse background and extensive training, Luis approaches coaching from a holistic and integrative perspective. He combines the wisdom of hypnosis, acupuncture principles, transpersonal psychology, and spiritual ministry to create a nurturing and transformative space for clients. Luis's empathetic and intuitive nature, combined with his vast knowledge and experience, allows him to support individuals in their personal, emotional, and spiritual growth with compassion, authenticity, and profound insight.

Has Anyone Seen My Soul?

Spiritually Transformative Experiences and the Discovery of Divinity

by Luis Melendez Jr.

When I first arrived in the United Kingdom in the spring of 1997, it was courtesy of the United States Army. I could not have been more thrilled to work alongside top civilian and United States Armed Forces personnel in what was, for my occupational specialty, a rare joint military operations assignment. However, little did I realize an extraordinary spiritual journey was poised to unfold by learning the sacred art of attuning to the Spirit World. By developing this profound connection, I discovered I could receive messages or visions from spirits to comfort the bereaved, feel the emotions or physical sensations of others, and channel healing power to aid the sick.

The psychic abilities described above are widely understood "mediumship" phenomena linked to many wisdom and religious traditions, as they involve communication between the human and spiritual realms. From ancient shamanic practices to the oracles of classical Greece, from spiritual healers in Indigenous communities to the modern Spiritualist movement, the concept of mediumship has manifested in diverse forms across time and cultures, highlighting its universal recognition and enduring significance. The wealth of psychical and scientific research bears witness to these profound religious experiences.

As a student of Spiritualism, I was captivated by Leonora Piper's remarkable ability to communicate with the spirit world through trance states, along with the incredible talents of other equally renowned mediums of the 19th and 20th centuries, such as Daniel Dunglas Home, Florence Cook, Eusapia Palladino, Mina Crandon, William Stainton Moses, and George Vale Owen. Their diverse abilities, ranging from levitation and materialization to direct voice communication and channelling of spirits and angelic beings, were integral parts of the rich tapestry of mediumship history. Witnessing modern-day mediums provide evidence of soul survival fuelled my desire to explore Spiritualism further, leading me to adopt a "rational," "scientific," and "experiential" approach to religion, which, up to that point, I didn't think was possible. The profound impact of these experiences prompted me to seek mentorship and dedicate myself to developing my mediumistic skills. In 2006, I felt prepared to answer the calling and begin serving Spiritualist churches.

The importance of academia to supplement spiritual understanding continued to evolve with my master's degree in transpersonal psychology and consciousness studies at the University of Northampton. Here, my focus shifted toward studying human potential. I became captivated by research that challenged conventional thinking, such as the fascinating findings on the brains of long-term meditators, which defied the notion of age-related deterioration. I also delved into controlled studies that measured the effectiveness of prayer interventions, comparing them to control groups of patients infected with HIV-AIDS. Additionally, I explored the realm of conscious control over out-of-body experiences, which became the subject of my thesis. This ongoing research gave me a broader perspective and deepened my appreciation for the limitless possibilities of human consciousness.

However, unbeknownst to me was the prevalence of similar and even more profound experiences happening spontaneously to people from all walks of life, *without any intention or training.* One particular case that struck me was that of my nephew, who, upon learning about my dissertation topic, confided in me about his own distressing encounters during sleep. He had been silently suffering from unexplained body paralysis, loud whistling sounds and heightened lucidity that accompanied his episodes, leading to a growing fear for his mental well-being. Little did he realize that his experiences were precursors to spontaneous out-of-body experiences, a phenomenon famously documented by Robert Monroe and others.

These experiences, often referred to as 'peak experiences,' 'exceptional human experiences,' 'anomalous experiences,' and now more broadly termed, **spiritually transformative experiences** (STEs), can occur as a result of prayer, meditation, ritual, psychedelic substances, or unexpectedly and can profoundly impact individuals, unveiling hidden facets of reality and providing glimpses into higher states of consciousness. Examples of STEs include **near-death experiences** (NDEs), where individuals report encounters with bright lights and a sense of being outside their physical bodies; mystical experiences, where individuals merge with the divine or experience profound oneness; encounters with deceased loved ones or spiritual beings, visions of future events, and sudden spiritual awakenings.

Consider the case of Brian Sadler who, while sitting next to his wife, Patricia, waiting to be served lunch at a charming village pub in Norfolk in 1983, became suddenly aware of a "shimmering" and "translucent" "white cloud" object hovering at the opposite end of the bar. It stood six feet tall and three feet wide and, to his complete amazement, began moving in his direction. Traveling around the tables—and not through them, this white cloud paused directly to his front before completely engulfing him. Brian goes on to say about the experience in his self-published book, *The Meaning and Purpose to Life—The Big Jigsaw Puzzle*:

> *"What happened next is difficult to put into words. At that instant, I became totally 'at one' with the Cosmos and knew every-*

thing there was to know. I knew the meaning and purpose of life. I knew the blueprint of life itself and that I (consciousness) was immortal and, in numerous forms, had always existed, and that 'death' was the great illusion of our physical world. I knew that everything from the smallest microbe to the largest galaxy is part of an incredible Cosmic Plan and that everything is linked. All is perfect and in accordance with a beautiful simplistic Law: the Law of Love.

"I knew that everything from the smallest microbe to the largest galaxy is part of an incredible Cosmic Plan and that everything is linked. All is perfect and in accordance with a beautiful simplistic Law—the Law of Love. That which we call 'evil' did not, and could not, exist at this level—neither does time as we know it. The radiation of peace and love was incredible, so much so that it was almost unbearable if that was possible. It was like a trillion volts of love—absolute bliss, total ecstasy. Earthly love is but a pale reflection by comparison."

Brian's experience is more in keeping with that of an advanced practitioner of Raj Yoga meditation, who develops the ability to quiet the mind, expand awareness, and access higher states of consciousness after many years of concentration, breath control, and self-inquiry practice. Brian's cosmic consciousness experience proved overwhelmingly positive and, in his words, "life changing." However, it would come at the cost of becoming hypersensitive to the cruel and unjust conditions of life on earth, making it difficult for him to settle down into everyday life. It took Brian a few years to recover, and he describes the great difficulty of adjusting afterward as follows:

"Suppose we took a poor, lonely, filthy, starving wretch—poor in health and clothed only in rags—from the gutters of Calcutta in India and instantaneously whisked him to some luxurious paradise island. There he was bathed, healed, and dressed in the most expensive clothes, given the best of food and drink, shown unconditional love by everyone there, told that this was his real home, that nothing would be too much trouble, just to ask if he needed

anything. Imagine him being in that new environment for a few weeks and absolutely ecstatic with happiness and security.

"One day the scene fades, and he wakes up clothed once more in his rags back in the gutters of Calcutta with all the filth and stench. How do you think he would feel? And how do you think he would explain it to others? Life for him would never be the same again. Before, he would have known no better, but now he does—much better."

Through my deep friendship with Brian and Patricia and my active participation in their philosophical discussion group for many years, I have been privileged to gain profound insight and solace by listening to the STEs shared by over 60 members. These conversations have significantly shaped my perspective, instilling in me the belief that individuals will eventually find the necessary resources and support to integrate their STEs. However, I have observed a growing number of individuals who cannot openly discuss their STEs, as they fear judgment, exclusion, and the negative labels that society may impose upon them. This chapter is dedicated to these courageous individuals who silently struggle with their experiences.

The STEs shared below hold a special place in my heart as they all come from my esteemed circle of family, friends, and acquaintances. I hope these stories will inspire readers to reflect upon their own experiences or those of others with heightened sensitivity and compassion. I also hope that by shedding light on these events, we can contribute to the eventual eradication of stigmatization surrounding STEs. Ultimately, my aspiration is that this collective exploration will prompt countless others to delve deeply into the spiritual dimension of life and contemplate its profound implications for us as individuals, as a society, and as a global community.

HEARING VOICES

In 2005, Luis Rodriguez, an Emergency Medical Technician, had a profound Spiritually Transformative Experience (STE) one day during work as follows:

"My partner and I were en route to Brooklyn College Hospital to transport a patient. While driving on the Brooklyn Queens Expressway and preparing to exit at Atlantic Avenue, our ambulance approached the ramp too fast and collided with the guardrail. The impact caused the ambulance to launch several feet upward before crash landing onto the adjoining oncoming traffic lane.

"While the ambulance was in mid-air, time seemed to freeze, and this overwhelming and all-consuming sense of dread gripped me. My entire world faded to black as countless scenarios of how I would die played out in my mind. Suddenly, a clear, distinct, and monotone voice resonated within me, stating unequivocally, 'Don't worry, you will be fine.' It was apparent that the voice did not belong to my partner, leading me to question if it was a figment of my imagination. Yet, I can say with exact certainty, upon hearing that voice, all fear instantly vanished.

"I was taken to the hospital, and a thorough examination revealed that my right leg was marred by deep bruises from my hip down to my knee. This discovery caused concern among the medical staff, who suspected internal bleeding. I was informed a surgeon would assess whether vascular surgery was necessary, plunging me into a bottomless pit of isolation and despair. Once again, time came to a halt, and in that instant, an inexplicable out-of-body experience engulfed me. It was as if I were an observer outside of myself, witnessing the situation as a medical staff member, facing the grim prospect of a patient—which happened to be me—potentially losing a limb. The feeling of dread was indescribable. However, shortly after that, the same clear, distinct, and monotone voice resounded again, assuring me, 'Don't worry, you'll be fine.' The out-of-body experience ended moments before

the surgeon returned to report no signs of internal bleeding to my tremendous relief."

In 2009, Davendra Singh, a home care assistant, had a similar STE while shopping at her local grocery. In her own words, she describes the experience as follows:

"One day, I went to the grocery store. While standing in line waiting to pay, I felt a heavy presence—it was a like a fear came over me. Suddenly, I heard a voice saying to me, 'Leave the Store—Get out Now.' I took it for nothing. Then again, I heard the same voice say, 'Leave Now.' I became nervous thinking I imagined this, and then again, I heard the same voice very clearly say, 'Get out.' A sudden fear came over me so I left the food there and went straight home. I felt that something was about to happen there —not knowing what. The next day I heard a gunman was there, and he robbed the deli. My immediate thought was it was God that protected me."

SEEING SPIRITS

Sales Coach Jess Reidell's first experience seeing spirits occurred when she was a child. Here's what she has to say about this encounter.

"When I was seven years old, I had a strange encounter where I saw two women spirits standing together in my closet. I remembered they looked similar, with one being slightly shorter than the other. They both had brown curly hair and were wearing white polo shirts. I remember my whole body stiffening up and feeling scared and paralyzed to speak or move, and I eventually went back to sleep. Fast forward 20 years, I travelled to Chattanooga, Tennessee for a personal training certification and checked in at a nearby budget hotel. While checking in, my room number was announced publicly in the lobby in the presence of several construction workers who were in a line behind me. In hindsight, I should have returned the key and have the front desk agent to try again without announcing my room number within earshot of

strangers, But I was 27 and naive, and was just hopeful that no one was paying attention and assured myself it wasn't a big deal. When I walked into my room at the cheap hotel with the outside entryway, I was shocked by how filthy and unpleasant it was considering the hotel had recently been taken under new ownership. I remember there was a cloth banner with a different hotel name hanging over the previous signage of the former hotel chain. The carpet was sticky, and the room had a funky smell, but I was determined to make the best of this experience as I was there to become a certified personal trainer so I could change careers.

"During the first night of the training, (which happened to be at a much nicer hotel that was way out of my budget) I struck up a conversation with a fellow participant, who happened to ask where I was staying. When I told her, her face turned white, and she hastily scribbled her phone number on a piece of paper and handed it to me, instructing me to give her a call "if I needed anything." This seemed odd, but at the time I didn't question why she would say that. Later that night, while studying for my test, the phone in my hotel room started ringing, but when I answered no one spoke on the other end. This happened a few times, so I eventually took the phone off the hook. I went to sleep and woke up at some point to see a spirit standing in the closet. Even though I had removed my contacts, I could see her kind facial expression. It appeared to be one of the same spirits I had seen 20 years ago. I was frozen, unsure of how to process this mentally. I closed my eyes, hoping she would disappear but when I reopened them, she remained. My entire body tensed up, and somehow, just like I had at the age of seven, I returned to sleep.

"In the early morning hours while it was still dark, I awoke again to hear banging on my hotel door. I was determined not to open it or communicate with whoever was on the other side of the door, as I didn't know anyone in the area and was staying alone in the room. Who has the nerve to go banging on a motel room door in the wee hours of a Sunday morning? It was unsettling. Eventually, the banging stopped. The next day at the workshop, the same girl who had given me her number asked me how my night went, and

80

matter-of-factly, I told her, 'I think I saw a ghost.' To my surprise, she responded by saying she didn't want to tell me this, but a couple from Canada had been abducted and murdered from that same hotel while it was under the previous ownership just a few weeks back.

"*Trying to piece together these events in my mind, I came to the conclusion that this spirit had been watching over me ever since I was a child. And by her presence that evening, she was there to remind me that she will continue to do so as a protector or guardian angel. I did end up complaining to the hotel management about the disgusting room. I also expressed concern about the public announcement of my room number, which was inappropriate and had put me in a vulnerable position. I asked for my money back and was refunded a portion of it. I remember my ex-husband whispering to me in a condescending tone while I was on the phone with the customer service rep from the hotel, 'Don't tell him about the* **GHOST.***' I saved a meme a couple of years back that still makes me laugh when I think of it, as it's so very true. It said, 'During the day I don't believe in ghosts; at night, I'm a little more open-minded.'*"

SOUL IMMORTALITY AND DIVINE REALIZATION

Neil Helm, in the delicate years of his childhood at the age of 5, underwent a profound near-death experience (NDE) that would shape his life in profound ways. Here's his personal reflection on this transformative encounter:

"*In August 1944, I was five years old and living on a farm/ranch along the North Dakota/Montana borders. My mother took my two older brothers (9 and 11 years-old) and me to assist a cousin (we thought of her as an aunt) in Central Montana who, as a female physician, contracted with the State of Montana to house, feed, and care for all palliative care patients. One afternoon, driving us from one hospital up into the Rocky Mountains where she maintained a TB sanatorium, my cousin turned off a rural road toward a barn-like structure, saying, "Let's take a swim." It was a natural hot springs that the local ranchers had dammed up to keep it at 100 degrees Fahrenheit, much like a hot tub. My cousin had a key to the structure, but in 1944, there were only two small lightbulbs for the large indoor swimming area. I was frustrated to see that my cousin, mother, and older brothers could all swim, whereas I had never been swimming before. However, I thought that I could swim, so I tried, and quickly failed. I remember distinctly gulping a final mouthful of hot water and thinking that drowning in this 100-degree water was going to be painful. I mentally prepared myself to die. In an instant, a profound peace and serenity came over me.*

"I had a fairly traditional NDE. I left my physical body and floated over a beautiful meadow filled with blooming flowers. I continued from the meadow across a pastoral lake and into a tunnel. I had absolutely no fear of the tunnel. I could see a light at the end of it. As I came out of the tunnel, the entire right wall was a light energy with a unique light that flowed over me like a misty waterfall. The light communicated to me, 'I am God.' I remember thinking or saying, 'Yes, sir.' After some time with the light flowing over me with feelings of complete peace, forgiveness, and love, the light communicated again, saying, 'It is not your time.'

"My spiritual body then returned to my physical body in the hot springs. My middle brother dove in and touched me, knowing no one was supposed to be under the water, and he pulled me to the edge of the pool. My physician cousin resuscitated me. That was a painful, somatic experience, going from the peace and serenity of being with God to the painful regurgitating of lungs full of hot water. As I lay on the edge of the springs some 30 minutes later, God came to me again and communicated that I did not need to share our experience with my conservative parents, who would call it a hallucination. God basically provided the inner knowing that I absolutely should not share my experience with my first-grade classmates as they (and their parents) would only think I was crazy by saying, 'Let's keep this to ourselves.' While I pondered it often, I did not share my experience for over 30 years, not until Moody's book in 1975 coined the term 'near-death ex-

perience,' and others then began to understand what I had been pondering in my heart for many decades.

"The NDE aftereffects are also reflected in my successful 40-year career in conducting research in government, corporate, and academic research centers. For example, early in my career, I was guided to provide humanitarian research and services. I conducted seminal research and early development on the use of space-based communications and GPS technologies for both disaster mitigation and search-and-rescue systems. I am pleased that these systems are still in use today and have been credited with saving many tens of thousands of lives. For this initial research and development, I was nominated for the Nobel Peace Prize."

EXPERIENCING MEANINGFUL COINCIDENCES

Maria Fernández, a university student, witnessed a significant coincidence on the tragic day of the Madrid train bombings, March 11, 2004. Here's her account of the event:

"I had spent months studying hard, putting all my effort into getting ready for university exams. But it seemed like everything was going wrong that day. At first, I started to feel uneasy and thought it was just my nerves acting up. I continued getting ready, but I started feeling physically unwell as time passed. I pushed forward and left home to the train station, each step became more and more exhausting, then more and more impossible. That's when I decided to turn back and go home. Later, when I turned on the TV, I couldn't believe what I saw—the train bombings had occurred.

"Since then, that experience has taught me so much about life and my purpose. I often wonder why I was spared that day. It made me realize how precious life is and how our choices can have a big impact. Now, I strive to live with intention, appreciate every moment, and make a positive difference in the lives of others."

Louise Kenny, an art teacher who worked part-time for Her Majesty's Prison Services, had a remarkable experience in 2015 that she perceives as a meaningful coincidence. Here's what unfolded:

"I had just finished an art therapy session at a residential home in the morning. After leaving the building, I went to my car, opened the passenger side door, and placed my bags inside with car keys on top. I started walking around the car (to get in driver's side) when the central locking system suddenly activated and locked all the doors.

"My spare keys were located 10 miles away, and fortunately, a kind staff member offered me a lift to my house. The delay meant I was already an hour late for other part-time work teaching art to prison inmates. Having now secured spare car keys and still determined to go to work, I proceeded before encountering heavy traffic. After sitting in traffic for nearly 45 minutes and going nowhere soon, I decided to return home and didn't think much about it.

"When I went to teach the next day, my colleagues informed me that I had been very lucky. There had been an incident at the prison the previous day. A fight had broken out, and the situation escalated, requiring many prison officers to be called to a particular wing. This left the teaching staff alone in a separate portable cabin. The two inmates I had were known to be difficult and non-compliant, requiring two officers to be always present. It would have put me in great danger if the officers had been pulled away.

"Reflecting on the events, I realized that I had owned the car for seven years and it had never locked itself before or after that day. The commute to work at the time of day in the early afternoon was typically easy and uneventful, with only occasional traffic delays of about five minutes. However, on that particular day, there was a severe accident involving emergency services, which was highly unusual for that time slot (1:30 p.m., non-rush hour).

I can't help but think that some higher force or fate prevented me from going to work that day."

Sonya Garcia, a bar manager based in Florida, experienced a significant event in 2014 when she dozed off while driving. Here's how she described her experience:

"That night, I was driving home from work. I had a few cocktails earlier and was exhausted. Everything happened so quickly, and the next thing I knew, I was startled by the loud noise of what seemed like bricks being thrown at my car. I remember being in the car with the seatbelt on. It then felt like someone had forcibly pulled me out. I attempted to seek help, but due to what I later discovered was a broken hip and a shattered disc, I couldn't walk and was in excruciating pain. It was late, dark, and I was somewhere in the woods. I couldn't see any signs of people or cars in the immediate area. I thought this was the end and prepared mentally to die in my sleep.

"The next thing I remember, a man appeared and kept talking to me. I remember him keeping me awake. Not sure how long he was there, but at some point, an air ambulance arrived, and I was transported to the hospital. My parents were notified and immediately came from New York to see me. I told them about the kind stranger who had stayed with me, and they wanted to thank him. Strangely, when we checked the police report, there was no mention of anyone else being present at the scene."

EXPANDED CONSCIOUSNESS AND UNITIVE EXPERIENCES

In 1998, at the age of 50, Jean Raza, a mother of two children, had a remarkable mystical experience. Here's her recollection of the event:

"I was traveling on the tube in London, a journey that I had undertaken many times. I was absorbed in my own thoughts when the train stopped at a station, and I looked up to see where I was.

A man entered my compartment, and as he sat down, I immediately recognized him. But it puzzled me how I knew him so well. I looked around the carriage and saw another face I recognized. This time it was a young black woman.

"I was just thinking it was an incredible coincidence when I happened to glance around the rest of the carriage and recognized all of the other passengers intimately and somehow felt a deep and loving connection with each and every one. I felt very uneasy about all of this, and panic started to set in. When the train arrived at my stop, I jumped up and made a quick exit out of the doors, not wanting to look at anyone in the process.

"I came out of the station and walked quickly down the road, and as I did so, I recognized and knew each face that passed me. I found this difficult to handle and tried to keep my eyes on the ground until I reached my destination. It took me a few days to come to terms with my experience as it had come unannounced and uninvited, but I felt so privileged to have had it. I have had this happen to me several times since and have gradually come to feel comfortable with it as well as a sense of love to all mankind."

In her own words, Joan Carra shares the profound story of her journey—a magnificent odyssey that encompassed radiant light, profound transformation, boundless love, unwavering hope, and the liberating power of forgiveness. Here's her vivid recollection of the spiritually transformative experiences that shaped her path:

"After I graduated from college and worked in radio in Vermont, I abruptly left when my grant to work in Public Radio was not renewed. This was before cable and the green mountains blocked the radio and television airwaves in that state.

"I was also in two car accidents as a passenger and was in a great deal of pain from whip lash and all over body aches. I came home Even though I was from New York, I was in cultural shock. My mother was dying of cancer and my father's business in the gar-

ment industry was being transferred to China. I was also in an abusive romantic relationship.

"I felt lost and even hypnotized.

"I was in so much confusion and pain that I thought of committing suicide. I reached for the pain killers I was prescribed for my accident but the thought if I didn't succeed and die, I would be adding more grief to what my family was going through with my mother's illness. I kept seeing myself in a hospital bed with my mother's eyes pleading why. Instead, I went back to my room, took out paper and I wrote a letter to God. I asked to be forgiven and asked who hypnotized me? I felt immoral and blinded in the horrible relationship I was in and I didn't understand how I had this compulsion and obsession which I thought was love, but it was so twisted.

"Six months later while I was in bed, I experienced a light that came from the top of my window in my bedroom in my childhood home. It was from the right window. I was on the second floor so it was not from a car light passing by. Then a second one came from the window opposite me. It actually entered in between the narrow space where the two shutters met. That one came forward and hit me between my eyes. The light was all loving, forgiving and I realized the oneness of all life. I even had a connection with a spider on its path, its life was just as important as mine as well as every other living creature. I now knew there was a high Divine force, and it renewed my soul. We are all interconnected. We are all loved. We are all forgiven.

"I saw God. I started to read the Bible and renewed my faith. Six months later I had a nervous breakdown and had flashbacks of a suppressed childhood memory of sexual abuse that happened outside my home. That person even reminded me of the boyfriend I was with before my breakdown. My psychiatrist said I had to relive my trauma in order to remember it.

"I was in therapy and took a temporary office job in NYC. I worked overlooking Central Park, was taught bookkeeping and they gave me a trip to their headquarters in Scotland.

"During this time, my mother's chemo medication was changed. One night, I got out of bed and went to the kitchen where my mother was sitting by the table. The room turned red and tilted. I had to hold on to the wall for balance. Then I saw my mother's hair fall out and her face became a skeleton. I knew she would die soon. With this round of chemo, she lost her hair and passed just like my vision. The doctor said she died from a side effect of the medicine.

"I had a bumpy road after this, my job relocated, and I bounced around. I was reading cards, just the 9 to the Ace of playing cards, the way my aunt did for friends. My day jobs were not working out and I started to get opportunities to do readings for clients and parties. I even got in the newspapers, magazines and in books recommending my psychic work. I focused on the positive and gratitude and attracted what I needed. I guided people with that message.

"An older psychic told me, the clients do not care about predictions, they just want you to share your strength.

"And that is what I do."

OUT-OF-BODY EXPERIENCES

In 1990, Scott Haslar, a law officer, encountered a profoundly life-altering event when he unexpectedly experienced an out-of-body experience during a highly controversial shooting incident. Here's his unique perspective on this transformative event:

"Unbeknownst to me at the time of the shooting, I was standing on what would later be proclaimed "sacred ground" as my dark journey began. Was it just plain coincidence, or a twist of fate

that directed me to that intersection of 10th Street and North College Avenue? I don't know the answer yet. In time, I may...

"*Before leaving for work that night, I had that gut feeling officers sometimes have. That feeling is hard to explain. I knew something out-of-the-ordinary was going to happen that night. Here in the big city, it was just another boring Sunday night. Despite my gut feeling, I wondered, what could possibly go wrong?... Later in the shift, the radio run was announced.*

"'*Attention all cars, attentions all cars. An armed robbery just occurred at the Taco Bell located at 6335 East 82nd Street,' the dispatcher announced. The suspect was a black male armed with a revolver who fled the scene of the robbery in a new red Chevrolet Camaro. The vehicle was located later and stopped. However, during the stop, the driver took off at a high rate of speed after several shots had been fired.*

"*During the lengthy on-again, off-again pursuit that reportedly reached speeds in excess of 80 mph, the suspect was able to skilfully elude other officers and dodge vehicles in his path for miles. Yet somehow, he lost control there, crashing right in front of me as I sat in my police vehicle, blocking traffic.*

"*As I ran toward the scene, I saw the suspect standing outside of the vehicle, but I never saw him get out of the car. I couldn't imagine how he managed that considering the severity of the crash.*

"*He then ran toward the Camaro and dove head-first into the driver's side window. I could only see his back and lower half at that point. I could no longer see his hands. I saw him throwing things around, as if he was searching for something. I thought I saw cash flying as he rummaged through the front seats.*

"*Searching. Searching for something.*

"*Suddenly, he just stopped. It looked like his arms came together, as if he grabbed something. My immediate thought was that* he located the gun he was armed with during the robbery. He glanced back until he made direct eye contact with me. He began pulling himself back out of the window.

"At that moment, I thought it was him or me. I fired, and in that split second, my life changed forever.

"That moment seemed like an eternity.

"It's hard to explain the situation from there. It's an experience that doesn't even make sense to me now. There, for a split second in time, I seemed to briefly come out of my body and watch the events unfold beneath me, all the while having some unexplainable understanding that I would survive.

"During my encounter with the suspect, I began to experience time in still frames and slow motion. Yet somehow, all movement within each frame seemed rapid. In that split second that I pulled the trigger, I was aware of being outside of my own body, seemingly detached or dissociated from it.

"Within that split second, it seemed, I was both observer and the observed.

"I was only aware I had fired when I noticed the smoke from the discharge of the firearm as it eerily raised skyward, backlit by the streetlamps. As normal processing of real-time events returned to me, so too did my hearing. I could hear things again that I didn't just seconds before, like the sirens of all responding vehicles.

"It was finally over. I was still alive."

SEEING JESUS

As Alexandra Leclere underwent craniosacral therapy for the first time, she was unexpectedly thrust into a realm of mystical wonder. The experience left an indelible mark on her psyche. Here's her reflection on this extraordinary occurrence:

"Gradually, I began to feel very mellow. After about 30 minutes, Hilarion was standing behind me, and I 'saw' Jesus Christ appear next to me, his sacred heart emanating a beautiful white light. He seemed to be offering me his heart and the beautiful light. I was overwhelmed. Jesus had long dark hair, a beard and a moustache, and was wearing a blue robe over a red tunic. He seemed to be surrounded by white light. The sight of him was so extraordinary that I was speechless. I felt encompassed by his light. My heart seemed to connect with his, and I entered a state of amazing bliss. I was calm and happy. Everything was perfect in the glory of that light.

"'Are you alright?' Hilarion questioned me. 'I see Jesus,' I whispered. 'He's offering me his sacred heart.' 'Oh,' Hilarion caught her breath. 'That's remarkable,' she said with feeling. 'Do you see him?' I whispered. 'No, I don't,' she answered. I could say no more. I wanted to stay forever in that beautiful presence of Jesus. It was pure, unconditional love. It seemed as though nothing else existed. Exhausted by the experience, I finally closed my eyes to rest. When I opened them again, Jesus was gone. I'm not Catholic, so I had no reason to imagine Jesus with his sacred heart. The image I saw wasn't even one that was familiar to me. I was astounded and transformed. The feeling of serenity, love, and well-being was overwhelming. It was beautiful and all-encompassing."

FINAL THOUGHTS

The spiritually transformative experiences presented in this chapter, in conjunction with the vast wealth of knowledge amassed over 150 years of psychical and scientific research on subjects such as mediumship, out-of-body experiences, psi phenomena, meditation, spiritual healing, the power of prayer, near-death experiences, end-of-life experiences, reincarnation, and mystical or unitive experiences presents compelling evidence supporting the existence of the soul. These extraordinary, unique, and profound encounters offer undeniable glimpses into elevated states of consciousness and a deep connection to something greater than ourselves.

In light of Occam's razor, a principle that favors simplicity and minimal assumptions when considering competing explanations, it is becoming increasingly apparent that the concept of the soul provides a coherent and elegant framework for understanding the nature of these experiences. This perspective recognizes that one aspect of our being belongs to the spiritual realm, while the other aspect belongs to the earthly realm, with the physical body serving as a vessel for the soul. By adopting this viewpoint, we can explore the profound implications of the soul's existence and its evolutionary journey, shedding light on the interconnectedness of our spiritual and earthly experiences.

Imagine, for a moment, if this understanding were widely accepted—viewing the human being through the lens of the soul's evolution. In such a world, it becomes apparent that psychic abilities are not mystical or supernatural phenomena at all but skills we have forgotten over time. They are inherent in human nature and await rediscovery and remembrance. Recalling past lives or reincarnation experiences, developing psychic abilities such as clairvoyance or telepathy, harnessing the power of thought to heal ourselves, or consciously inducing out-of-body experiences to explore the mysteries of the universe would be recognized as natural and valuable skills, just like any other.

Furthermore, the proliferation of spiritually transformative experiences could also be interpreted as a profound awakening of humanity, a sign of a more significant shift in consciousness that various wisdom traditions throughout history have predicted. These traditions, not limited to Christianity alone, have foretold the reappearance of enlightened beings, such as Christ, who would guide humanity toward a new era of spiritual understanding and unity. The abundance of spiritually transformative experiences could indicate that this future event draws closer as more individuals awaken to the truth of their spiritual nature and the interconnectedness of all beings. It is a time of great potential and possibility, where the integration of spiritual experiences becomes a catalyst for personal and collective transformation, leading us toward a more enlightened and harmonious world.

To book your free consultation with Luis, please visit:

https://www.hypnosisworks.nyc/

https://www.silencespeaks.tv/

REFERENCES:

Alvarado, C. S. (1989). *Trends in the study of out-of-body experiences: An overview of developments since the nineteenth century.* Journal of Scientific Exploration, 3(1), 27-42.

Bucke, R. M. (1923). *Cosmic consciousness: A study in the evolution of the human mind.* EP Dutton.

Doyle, A. C. (2022). *The history of spiritualism.* Open Road Media.

Fenwick, P., Lovelace, H., & Brayne, S. (2007). *End of life experiences and their implications for palliative care.* International Journal of Environmental Studies, 64(3), 315-323.

Haslar, S. L. (2022). *On Sacred Ground: Death, Trauma, and Transformation: Memoir of an Officer Involved Shooting.* (n.p.): BookBaby.

Helm, N. (2018). *The Effects of Near-Death Experiences on Religious and Spiritual Beliefs.* (Publication No. 10843744) [Doctoral dissertation, Sofia University]. ProQuest Dissertations and Theses Global.

James, W. (1936). *The Varieties of Religious Experience: A Study in Human Nature.* United Kingdom: Modern library.

Kason, Y. (2019). *Touched by the Light: Exploring Spiritually Transformative Experiences.* Canada: Dundurn Press.

Leclere, A. (2005). *Seeing the Dead, Talking with Spirits: Shamanic Healing Through Contact with the Spirit World.* United States: Inner Traditions/Bear.

Luders, E., Cherbuin, N., & Gaser, C. (2016). *Estimating brain age using high-resolution pattern recognition: Younger brains in long-term meditation practitioners.* Neuroimage, 134, 508-513.

Maslow, A. H. (1994). *Religions, Values, and Peak-Experiences.* United Kingdom: Penguin Publishing Group.

Melendez, L., Jr. (2016). *"There is nothing to fear about dying. This Earth is not our home and what lies beyond is marvellous.": An IPA exploration of the out-of-body experience - single participant case study.* (Master's dissertation, University of Northampton).

Monroe, R. A. (1992). *Journeys Out of the Body: The Classic Work on Out-of-Body Experience.* Harmony.

Moody, R. A. (2001). *Life after life.* Random House.

Owen, G. V. (1921). *The Life Beyond the Veil: Spirit Messages Received and Written Down by the Rev. G. Vale Owen... with an Appreciation by Lord Northcliffe and an Introduction by Sir Arthur Conan Doyle...* Ed. by HW Engholm (Vol. 1). George H. Doran Company.

Sadler, B. (2011). *The Meaning and Purpose of Life: The Big Jigsaw Puzzle.* United Kingdom: Bloomsbury Publishing Plc.

Sicher, F., Targ, E., Moore 2nd, D., & Smith, H. S. (1998). *A randomized double-blind study of the effect of distant healing in a population with advanced AIDS. Report of a small-scale study.* Western Journal of Medicine, 169(6), 356.

Smith, M. D. (Ed.). (2014). *Anomalous experiences: Essays from parapsychological and psychological perspectives.* McFarland.

Stevenson, I. (1980). *Twenty cases suggestive of reincarnation.* University of Virginia Press.

Laura Cooke

Leave It All On The Dancefloor:
Why it's never too late to follow your dreams

To purchase a signed paperback copy of the book, get an e-book version, or join our community

Do you feel like you were meant for more? Are you afraid of wasting this precious life by staying small?

Do you know what's getting in your way of taking that first step towards your dreams or even knowing what that dream is?

Since I was a small child, I had a deep knowing that I was meant to make a difference in this world. The worst part is, I had NO clue what that meant or what I was supposed to do.

THE FIRST STEP TAKES COURAGE

Since then, I have been painfully searching, trying and failing, and numbing when things went wrong. It was a battle between the knowing I was meant for more, and the gut-wrenching disappointment within each thing I tried and failed at, over and over again. **These are not small failures.**

WHAT I'VE COME TO REALIZE

I've always been a seeker, a lifelong learner, and I enjoy digging into new ways of being challenged.

I now know that my purpose and journey was to travel that heartbreaking road of striving, falling down, and getting back up to help others avoid some of the tough lessons I had to learn the hard way.

That's why I wrote this book that outlines all of my learnings, into resources and tools to help you find your story and succeed on your path to fulfilling your purpose.

Along the way, you'll read the amazing stories of 23 women who have transformed their lives, overcome extreme hardship, and found their purpose. I can't wait for you to start this journey so you can write YOUR story of overcoming and success.

Ritu Chopra

Technologist, Executive Coach, Author, International Speaker, Award-winning Film Director

RITU CHOPRA, a technologist by profession, is an author, TV show host, award winning film producer, a certified leadership coach, and international speaker who is on her spiritual journey.

With 25+ years of experience in Fortune 500 companies serving in IT operations, information security in global financial, & health care industries,

Ritu now mentors and coaches emerging leaders to achieve their "Personal Mastery." She is Founder of **Lead My Way**, a Not-for-Profit Org, and a passionate advocate

of Women Leadership and Empowerment Initiatives. Her recent book 'Women Leadership in the 21st Century, Creating and Raising Leaders of Tomorrow' is another example of her dedication to helping women.

This book is an important and timely message about Women's role in the workplace and societies today worldwide.

PROGRAMS AND COURSES RITU OFFERS:

- Self-Discovery to Self-Mastery
- Women Leadership in 21st Century
- Mindfulness for Stress Reduction

Judith Juhnke

Transformation Coach & Business Mentor for Visionary Female Entrepreneurs, Speaker, Author. Judith is a starseed from Germany, home in the world. She shares life for 20+ years with her soulmate and husband Daniel. In her heart beat the drums of revolution and challenge likewise the sweet voice of nurturing and love which both are deeply reflected in her holistic work. Judith holds a degree in Intern. Business + Mgt, 3 coaching certifications and has opened her soul gifts of channeling and light language.

Purpose-Frequency: Creating Success the Joyful Way

Five Paradigm Shifts in Running Your Business in the New Earth Era

by Judith Juhnke

Are you sometimes wondering why your life and business still feel harder than you wish?

Do you also question if you really belong here in this life?

I was at odds with both. When I was younger, I didn't understand it; it was "packaged" in a deep feeling of not belonging anywhere and having to fight for and against everything. I went on a quest thinking I needed to prove to the world I could do it MY way.

I had no clue what that really meant :)

I learned that the real quest was to prove my power and worthiness to myself and to find my own voice back. When I started to embody it deeply, my true soul's purpose-frequency and identity unfolded.

Let me take you on a journey of self-discovery and self-mastery that will enable you to create success in your business with joy connected to your purpose-frequency.

Today I'm standing in the space as a successful coach and entrepreneur for "new earth" purpose-led business that matches the consciousness & frequency of the new earth era where we create, market and sell in a new way: from Soul2Sale.

The new earth era means we include multi-dimensionality, the quantum field and deep sensing into all creation processes. That leaves logic, linearity and rationality behind.

Moving from one into the other can create anxious feelings and self-doubt if you are really doing the right thing. While at the same time you just **KNOW** that thing is true for you. It is a funny thing. Can you resonate?

That feels like starseeds or lightleaders in the house and maybe you are wondering how you can bring it all together in your business: the inner knowing of your truth and the outer online business space that tries to tell you how you should do marketing and sales.

The secret is: the 2021 marketeers don't know either. ;) This is a fully new space that you get to trailblaze in. But there's guidance in this book.

Let me share a bit more of my story before we go into the five paradigm shifts to connect with your purpose-frequency and integrate 5th dimension wealth in your business with joy. Little spoiler alert here: you need YOU at full soul level and that might be equally scary and/or blissful along the way.

My life journey started like this: I was born a Sunday girl in a small village in the north of Germany full of light and joy. I grew up in a house with my parents, both mid-level state attorneys, my younger brother and my grandparents who were traditional working-class people. Everyone tried their best, yet the energies of lacking self-love, mistrust, scarcity, and violence were present. My uncle owned a farm, and my aunt worked in a bookstore. The ideas of being financially wealthy, creating success or discussing business ideas were foreign concepts from another planet. We only knew hard work to make ends meet. I can safely say that I wasn't born an entrepreneur, and maybe you weren't either. But it's time to look beyond what the eye can see.

Don't get me wrong, we had amazing times. My parents organized the best kids' birthday parties with fun games in the garden or the nearby forest, and I loved spending holidays on the farm running in the fields and playing with the piglets and my cousins.

But in a period of about three years, everything changed for me, and it took me 33 years to connect the dots and another three years to get to where I am today writing this book having served more than 250 clients as a coach and mentor in their evolution into their soul's purpose and success.

My war-traumatized grandfather had struggled his whole life with love, and the outlet he and some fellow men found was to "share" this unexpressed "love" and "desire" with kids. The "sharing" one day got so intense that I almost died with some man's hands around my throat. Before turning six, I took all my courage to tell my parents what was happening. They didn't have the capacity at that time to hear the truth, God bless them. I wasn't believed to tell the truth.

I started to believe that I didn't have a voice, that it wasn't safe to be me and to show my feminine side so I cut my hair short at age seven and refused to wear dresses and tights anymore. I thought I wasn't worth being heard and seen. My light and joy shifted to rage and suffering.

Not being believed by my parents got me so traumatized that I didn't remember what happened until 33 years later as a grown woman. Through my personal development journey, the full memory came back. The universe decided "she's now ready to handle it."

And I was. A profound healing and evolution journey started faster than I could have ever imagined and in perfect alignment with the ascended frequencies and consciousness of the planet. For a while, my grandfather's soul has even been on my spiritual team until our learning journey was complete.

It takes surrender and trust to allow experiences like this to let you look at yourself and how a gift can unfold unexpectedly.

I sit in deep breathwork, fully drifting in space, connected to my inner wisdom.

Suddenly, I notice a person appearing.

Now I see him: a young version of my now dead grandfather.

He apologizes for all he had done to me. I allow the words to reach my heart.

A deep sense of forgiveness starts to unfold within me. Slow and gentle tears are running down my cheeks. I smile and keep breathing. In and out.

What is happening next blows my mind. Behind my grandfather a huge group of men gathers. They look at me. Next, they all kneel and bow. Now I understand: the group is everyone who had been involved back then in this game of "sharing love" with me and other kids. I sense their sincere soul-apology for all the pain and suffering they caused and them being sorry that, in their human version, they were in this role.

I am standing and allowing forgiveness to open up. Tears of relief and joy run down my face. My body shakes off trauma, my arms and legs are moving. I keep breathing. I let go. The cycle is closed. I reclaim another piece of my soul's freedom. I can forgive because I can see how my "not dying" when I almost did had massively built my strength to never give up. On purpose.

And even more important, I feel how it meant stepping into my power to win no matter how hopeless a situation may seem.

From then onwards, my grandfather's soul supported me in seeing my truth in my evolution journey with special focus on the business and what my audience needs to hear next in posts, emails and video. What an epic and unexpected "coach" simply because I had allowed and trusted.

Your own healing and evolution journeys are always connected to something in your business. It's never two separate things, and the reason why only focusing on strategy in your business doesn't get you those soul-aligned clients and sales, but rather gets you stuck in your head chasing the answer to why it's not working. We get to bring in multidimensional connections starting with trusting ourselves again at deeper levels.

Despite the intense experiences I had as a child, I deeply believe that everything happens for a reason. It holds our purpose, lets us master our strengths, and helps us develop our big vision and mission for this lifetime. As starseeds and visionaries, we get to express through our businesses. I always say that your business is an expression of your soul's purpose.

Pure strategy and blueprints are tools of the past, yet you want orientation and a structure to build and grow a business to make it feel lighter and less overwhelming.

What I found works well for me and my clients is a framework that works like a buffet:

You just take what serves at the time you need it. That means enough structure to feel safe and enough freedom to find exactly YOUR way.

The Purpose-Wealth-Cosmos I created over the past three years guides lightleader and starseed entrepreneurs to their purpose-frequency and to a successful business and life where they express themselves without trying to fit in any blueprint.

Let's dive in and discover how you can connect to your pur-pose-frequency and lead your business with joy the new earth way. I've broken it down into five paradigm shifts

PARADIGM SHIFT #1
ADVERSITY HOLDS YOUR BIGGEST STRENGTHS AND THE CONNECTION TO YOUR PURPOSE-FREQUENCY

As someone who has experienced and healed from deep trauma, I have a strong desire for freedom, individualization and finding MY way. I wanna be guided by a mentor, not be told what to do so I can trailblaze and form these new pathways. Do you resonate with that?

That's the pure purpose of pioneers, visionaries, lightleaders and starseeds: walk and create outside the existing lines.

The thing is that it takes power and courage to live such a purpose. And that power and courage needed to be built somehow in this lifetime. If you were the universe, what would you send someone if you wanted to "train" courage and power?

Right. Difficult situations to overcome.

That is what is called trauma experiences: situations that have been so emotionally overwhelming that you fall into coping mecha-nisms to protect yourself.

Down to losing memory for a certain period of time like in my case.

There is a two-fold beauty in trauma-experiences:

1. Your coping mechanisms unconsciously "train" your strengths. For example, healthy adult empaths can read you emotionally within milliseconds to see how they can support you because when they were little, they most likely had an environment (e.g., alcoholic or narcissistic parent) that they constantly

needed to scan to see if it was safe to show up or to ask for something.

This accounts for me as well, even though I didn't remember consciously what happened. Where I grew up, a mix of passive-aggressiveness and pleasing others was present. It is the magick and power of the subconscious and unconscious mind that guides your behavior and you can learn how to use this power in your favor to create.

We have five core strengths that will show up most in our behavior. Becoming aware of them supports creating a solid base in your business. I will talk about that later in more detail.

2. Your biggest adversity holds your purpose. It might feel a bit odd to be diving deeper into what has been the hardest and most painful thing you have experienced. Yet by allowing to see the truth in it, you not only heal the pain, but get clarity on the big Why in your life; the away-from-motivation from which you derive your vision as the go-to-motivation

   Looking at trauma work, positive psychology, emotion science, energetics and neuroscience, I found that there is a correlation between visionary people who see and sense solutions and ideas outside the existing structures and norms and the level of traumatizing events they've experienced in their lives.

The newest "surprise" that comes with the higher levels of consciousness and frequency is that after healing the trauma, finding purpose and belonging, the ancient innate super-sensory skills awaken in each of us. Like psychic gifts, clairvoyance or channelling light language.

When you match your purpose with this "new" side of skillset inside, the true paradigm shift and the revolution is birthed in how we create success and wealth while serving the world: **You create from your purpose-frequency**.

Connected to the earth and to your ancient home of your soul in the galaxies.

Now the perceived confusion around where you belong got a new perspective, right?

PARADIGM SHIFT #2
WALKING OUTSIDE THE LINES: SELF-CONFIDENCE, BABY

Have you felt like the rainbow sheep of the family, the one that no one "gets"? Me, too. Love that you're here and guess what—you were never meant to fit in.

A huge aha-moment for me was to understand that "to embody being different" just means "being me." Because of my childhood experience, I had no idea what "being me" could look like. My standard answer to any question of "Judith, what would you want XYZ to be like for you?" was "Umm, I don't know." I couldn't even decide what I wanted from the menu in a restaurant. Every decision that included my personal desires felt unsafe.

The tricky thing is, how you do one thing, you do everything. Not being able to make clear decisions when it came to me personally wasn't a good baseline to become a successful entrepreneur with a personal brand. I was great with making decisions as long as it wasn't about my personal choices, thus the thriving career under the umbrella of corporate organizations until I got told one too many times that my ideas and concepts were too far out, too innovative and didn't fit the global strategy.

When I started my own business journey, I tried to operate in the same system I knew from the corporate world, mixing it up with strategies for online marketing I found on the internet. Kinda funny to think that it would work when I look back now.

Everything you need to know is held in the inner intelligence of your soul and DNA. The question is: Do you feel safe enough to access it and on top, to express it? I didn't, but understood that I had to find a way.

Conquering what felt like a mountain the size of the Alps to me, was to get to the embodiment that it's safe to express all of me in all my light and all my dark. The path led me to re-learning how to feel ALL emotions and discover that fun wasn't joy. And to finding and loving my feminine side and integrating the divine feminine power within.

Achieving this requires balancing and mastering what I call the **Human Side** of you.

That is your mind, your thoughts, your emotions, and your body, specifically your nervous system.

1. You heal and balance all the "old sh**" by creating balance in life and flowing with the waves as they come.
2. Mastery comes when you experience an expansion of consciousness in contrast to healing old wounds.

The bliss of this expansion does come with a new challenge: With every growth step, a deeper and more delicate version of resistance patterns comes to the surface wanting to stop you from walking further outside the lines into the unknown.

And it also means, you get to dance the beautiful dance with fear and find the truth in it every time you walk over the edge again.

PAST — BALANCING: HEALING OLD WOUNDINGS

FUTURE — MASTERING: GROWTH + EVOLUTION

Next, I dive into how you get there.

PARADIGM SHIFT #3
BALANCING AND MASTERING YOUR HUMAN SIDE

Let's walk through all three areas of the Human Side so you get a clear picture of what it means for you and your business. This is how you connect to your high vibrating purpose-frequency.

A) **EMOTIONS:** Release the shame to be different to most and embrace the fear to be excluded when seen and heard in all light and power

What most people don't know (even in the spiritual space) is that every emotion has a function. It is supposed to tell you something. When you feel stress, that is your emotion in dysfunction. I loved learning the neuro-science part of it when I got certified as Emotion Coach.

As most entrepreneurs can relate to this, we look into shame and fear coming up once we desire to be more visible and embody our true self, the emotions tell us the following:

SHAME: the function of shame is to provide you with the ability to feel sorry and apologize when you did something that was not okay, so that you don't get "rejected" by your tribe.

I felt unconsciously ashamed to show up with my vulnerable and juicy feminine side, and it showed up in procrastinating about things in my business. It was connected with thoughts of "people might laugh at me when I post this" or "what if someone finds out, I'm actually not the real deal?

Can you see how the trauma-experience of my parents not believing me when I was little played out here in a beautiful way for me to look at it and heal it?

What happens underneath is this: the dissonance pattern in which you are operating "tells" you constantly that because you did something wrong in the past and you got "excluded", it's gonna happen again every time you try to be you. So, you hesitate to say what you want to say.

FEAR: the function of healthy fear is to get you to determine if you considered all relevant factors when discovering something new and in case something needs to be adjusted, to provide the energy to implement it. You see, fear is a good friend that will keep you safe WHILE moving ahead.

The dissonance pattern underneath "tells" you that you don't have the power to actually do it, so you should stop trying (and just chill) or to analyze why you're not getting there even though logically, the path is so clear.

I had this pattern deeply ingrained in my identity, and one way it showed up for me was my language. It shocked me when I realized how many times my sentences included "I can't". That was one huge reason my manifesting processes felt so hard and broke off a lot; the old "I can't" identity was 100% disconnected from my high vibrating purpose-frequency.

Both emotions described in their dysfunctional state are a version of survival and a reason to feel stuck and not implementing. As a result, you might feel frustrated, disappointed or powerless about not expressing all your wisdom in your marketing and not making sales.

One thing I teach my clients to create more balance is to start activating and growing their emotional super resources of pride, gratitude, relaxation and awe.

Want to know a secret? The 2018 version of me used to say with conviction "I am not afraid of anything." That was before I understood that I had largely disconnected from feeling at all and that my biggest fear was being seen and heard in my full light and power. That was a harsh moment of raw truth.

B) **NERVOUS-SYSTEM:** Surrender to being in discomfort and not knowing HOW. You need a healed nervous system to create success and influence.

Your body holds the memory of all events of this life and your past lives in the cell memory or your DNA. Connected to these memories is always the energetic trace of a feeling that feels either comfortable or uncomfortable.

A highly dysfunctional nervous system in constant survival mode is not only exhausting, it also blocks the access to your beautiful divine, feminine awakened consciousness and your purpose-frequency to create and manifest with ease and flow anything you desire. And it disconnects you from access to your super-sensory skills.

Signs pointing to survival mode are:

- anxiety, not fully breathing in and out or even unconsciously holding your breath,
- slow or no bowel movement, and
- fake high-performance aka hustling to keep you busy and productive.

I embodied with a level of mastery all the above without noticing for the longest time and thinking that the way I felt and operated was normal.

When I re-learned to fully breathe in and out and allowed myself to take up more space, it was a wild trigger of fear and panic. My nervous system went into full alert, reminded of the past, where being too present and seen meant danger and suffering.

This "mechanism" caused me to play at surface level with my content when I started marketing myself online. My content was entertaining, but it wasn't converting. People just watched, but didn't really connect to ME. In 2019, it still worked to some extent and

I got clients here and there. In 2023, it is a full breaker if your content can't reach a certain depth, value and proof of authority infused with authentic and aligned shares of YOU.

I learned to regulate my nervous system and to retrain the cell-memory. I changed the default response to unknown situations through breathwork and neuro-somatic movements that release trauma memory from the body.

As entrepreneurs that's gold as we move into new, unknown situations all the time, right? That's why this has also become part of what I'm teaching.

I personally had the wildest experiences when breaking through the discomfort and finding peace. I reintegrated my divine feminine and my divine masculine this way. On top of that every experience created an opportunity to share from the classroom and to finetune my marketing.

C) **MIND:** Claim back your power by going from a reacting suffering identity to responding as the multidimensional light leader you are

You may have heard that your reality is as you choose to see and embody it: Happiness, success, money, freedom, wealth, satisfaction, bliss, lifestyle, business … every .. single … thing.

The major shift that changes every single thing is training your awareness and how your "mind is set" from reacting to a situation (victim consciousness) to responding to a situation (flow consciousness).

My default reacting pattern used to be fight and struggle. A part of me sensed potential danger and thus I created a reality of lots of fight and struggle. Up to finding myself in a street fight in Havana in 2011 when two men tried to rob us.

Through the inner work I have done, I found peace, flow, trust and presence. I want to share with you what that looks like in action with the next powerful story:

It's February 2023 in Mexico. I walk to the supermarket to get water at 9:30 p.m., a 5-minute walk. I'm walking and feeling grateful for all the amazing experiences and the love Mexico has shown me. A man on a bike passes me. He mumbles something. I am not paying attention. I hear him talking behind me and turn around. The part of the roadway is darker. Next, I hear him saying, "We need to make love. Come here." There are several meters distance between us.

I think, *Fuck, this can't be true*. I am fully present and clear. I say, "No, I don't think so" and keep walking faster. He passes me with the bike and blocks the way repeating, "We need to make love." He then tries to touch me.

I see him; he is 45-50 years old, significantly smaller than me and probably from the area. I am fully present holding his gaze. I push him off and shout out loud and decisively, "Do not touch me!" in Spanish. I move on.

He gives me a slap on the shoulder and backs off, slightly irritated. I keep walking fast. Twenty seconds later, I reach the next corner, full of streetlights. Other people walk by chatting. I look down the road. He is gone. I keep walking to the supermarket, buy my bottle of water and walk the same way back home.

Was I scared? Yes, but I didn't panic. I stayed calm and present. Did I have funky thoughts? Oh yes.

My mind went from, *How can this happen just a second after I felt so grateful for all the kindness I have experienced the last three weeks to what am I sending out that this man apparently resonated with and acted the way he did?*

When I was back home, I let myself feel what was coming up. I breathed into my lower back and hip area, which had gotten tense, and I observed myself asking the question inside, *what do I choose to make this mean?*

- I will not let 5 minutes of my month in Mexico change how I view all other experiences that have been full of support, love and kindness. *I am choosing to feel safe and supported here.*

- I proved to myself my power in a situation where when I was 4-6 years old, I had no power to escape the violence my body and soul received. Today, I stayed fully in the moment, connected to myself. *I am powerful, and it's safe to show it.*

- I could feel the desperate search for love of his soul underneath his violent actions. And I could sense his inner conflict; he knew what he did wasn't right. I could sense the shame, while he so desperately longed for physical touch and love that this part won over the other in that moment. But because of that, I was sure he wouldn't wait around the corner. *I trusted myself, I can shift perspectives, and I trust my inner wisdom.*

Obviously that identity shift didn't happen overnight for me, yet I wanted to share it with you as this level of trust and consciousness is what enables you to fully lean into your business when the going gets tough.

That is where no strategy or positive affirmation will get you ahead and to the next sale, but deep transformation of who you believe to be will. Take a deep long breath in and out, then keep reading.

PARADIGM SHIFT #4
EXPRESSING YOUR MULTI-DIMENSIONALITY WITH CONFIDENCE AND ACTIVATING YOUR SOUL SIDE

Let's look at the "woo woo" side of you. I want to directly reframe this term. It is frequently used in the online space to describe the non-logical, non-strategic side of success stories. I'm bold enough to unleash the power behind the term "woo-woo." In my space we're talking about magick of energetics, multidimensional abilities and purpose-frequency. It is what makes you unique and it's your best unique selling proposition (USP). So instead of watering it down, we will shout it from the rooftops.

Ready to discover your **Soul Side** as an equal element to your Human Side? It requires activation and remembrance for you to access the answers to all questions about your life and business.

A) **REMEMBERING PIONEER WISDOM:** This is your ancient inner wisdom you carry in your DNA and in your soul. It stems from all past lifetimes and your ancestral lineage and is a pool of pure knowing once it is unlocked. It shows up as what you might know as the 6th sense, your intuition or those moments when you just know, but cannot explain why. This doesn't happen accidentally. When you start practicing to listen to these impulses, you will find that solutions and ideas come way easier than you could ever create them through logical thinking. It is an unlearning process of how you get to a result as society is only teaching us to go with logic and rationality. Your true power lies in your wisdom. It is more powerful than your brain when it comes to decision making and knowing your truth.

Why train to remember it now? Your soul has chosen to come back down to earth for a reason. Its ancient wisdom is in high demand in this time of planetary transformation and you get to rediscover and fully express it. That's part of your purpose.

For full leverage in your business, you need your purpose-frequency. It resonates at your highest timeline and is your key to manifesting into earth reality the multi-faceted wealth and abundance you see, sense and know deep inside.

Through my awakening I got to understand that my soul carries a portal between the spiritual realms and earth life. We are not supposed to cut one off; it's about uniting both.

A great way to start intentionally connecting to your pioneer wisdom is playful curiosity. Connect inside with a question like asking your body how it wants you to move it and practice listening to the answer. In my work, I use frequencies, sounds, visual stimulation and movement infused in breathing journeys to enhance and activate your connection to the deeper creative levels of your subconscious mind. This is how I connected to my purpose-frequency and created my first 5 figure cash month.

B) **ACTIVATING YOUR HIGHER SELF AND AWAKENED CREATIVE CONSCIOUSNESS**

You have skills and abilities that are 100% outside of logic. Your **Soul Side** is claiming back its equal share of creation from heart, soul and the conscious creative mind.

It again requires trust to fully express it as it may be very "alien" skills compared to your human strengths. I encourage you to allow your X-Woman to show up (think like in the X-MEN movies): Speak Fairy Language, Channel from the Arcturian or Andromedan People, Open Portals with Crystals, Jump Timelines, Co-Create with the Universe. Discover who you truly are. Where your starseed or lightleader soul's origin is.

I found the easiest way to bring my soul side more into my everyday reality by approaching it with the curiosity of a child and with daily practice. I'm teaching my clients how to do this as one part of the Purpose-Wealth-Cosmos I created. For me since the beginning of this year, light language and light codes have come through; some people also call that sound healing. It is a revolution in communication: information is conveyed through sound, signs, movement or drawings that directly speak to your soul. Your brain doesn't understand, but your soul will.

Want to know another secret? When light language wanted to come through for me, I first had experiences where my jaw would move like predators chewing through prey, opening wide and moving in funny ways in all sorts of directions. Plus, I was making sounds like dogs, wolves and lions as well. That definitely felt "alien."

Another way I am receiving messages is channelling codes, energies and messages, e.g., from the Arcturian people through hand movement or into my awareness so I can just say what I receive and pass it onto the person it's meant for. For you, it can look similar or you may find your psychic abilities opened up like fully seeing into someone's energy field across timelines and dimensions or channelling answers to every specific question.

Embrace this part of you with love, gratitude and curiosity and allow it to guide you in your business decisions.

C) STAY CONNECTED AND BRIDGE THE GAP

What I see a lot of light leaders, starseed business owners and visionary entrepreneurs struggle with is this: You discover and connect to the gifts, abilities and power of your Soul Side.

You love it, it feels so peaceful, harmonious and naturally at home that you want to stay there in this 5D experience of expanded consciousness and you struggle to understand what this means now for how you do business and life overall. You might find yourself stuck, wanting to move, but not knowing how.

Your purpose-frequency is the connection line to express from one world into the other.

What happens when you feel stuck between both worlds, is in reality a simple reaction of your Human Side:

Your brain feels overwhelmed and scared by these new illogical ways of communicating and creating, which it cannot understand. So, it does what it can do best—it brings up fear and creates the illusion for you that there is a gap in the form of time between the present moment in 3D and what wants to come here in the form of 5D. You get stuck in your head trying to figure out the solution for how to bridge it. Since there is no solution as there is no gap, you go in circles.

The truth is, both IS now, and you just need to focus back into your body into the here and now, allowing your human side to relax and connect back to your purpose-frequency. Remember that I said in paradigm shift #2 that once you reach more expansion than healing, the self-sabotage patterns get more creative.

PARADIGM SHIFT #5
NEW EARTH BUSINESS: SELL YOUR SOUL'S PURPOSE

Let's look at your business now leading from your purpose-frequency and using your strengths from your Human Side and your Soul Side. It's easier than you think.

Remember that your business is an expression of your soul's purpose. You get to be paid limitlessly for being of service with your strengths and soul magick by packaging it in your offers, programs and services while you enjoy life to the fullest.

A new dimension calls for a new approach. So, I shift the paradigm and say, *don't look at the market to find your niche, audience and brand identity.*

For two reasons:

1. The existing market is largely a reflection of the past. Even if "past" here relates to just one year ago. You are about to create something from the here and now and beyond what exists. The only thing you need first is YOU and full balance and mastery of your Human Side and activation and remembrance of your Soul Side.

2. With ascended frequency and consciousness of the planet and humankind, we are moving through evolution faster than ever, and the shift that has come in 2023 is so big compared to 1 or 2 years ago that those strategies and ways of creating something just don't work anymore. You truly get to create into the unknown with trust and confidence. That's the freedom your soul is craving for and that your mind fears at the same time.

To navigate with more ease & joy into 5th dimension success, I have created a new way to reach the most soul aligned people: Reverse engineer your business foundation based on your strengths and your purpose. This makes you completely independent from any market conditions as you could launch aligned products in any environment at any time because it all roots in your soul's purpose and that doesn't ever change.

The business part of my Purpose-Wealth-Cosmos is called the "SOUL2SALE" framework, which is divided into two parts. The first one delivers your niche, ideal audience, brand message and your offers. In a nutshell, these 9 steps will create the foundation of your business:

1. Define your top 5 strengths

2. Become aware of the blind spot of each strength

3. Understand what strengths and blind spots look like in action and belief system for you. Your strengths in action are what your soul-aligned audience sees in you and what they desire; your blind spots in action represent your audience's struggles and pain points

4. Timeline back the action patterns of the blind spots to your biggest adversity = your purpose

5. From your purpose (why) = "away from" develop the "go to" vision = what instead in feeling, identity and result = that's your niche

6. Take the core of your emotional and belief system struggle (A) and the desired result in feeling (B) and for both, the conse-

quences manifests in reality when you are in A or B = this is your most aligned audience's struggle and desire at their core

7. Add outer context to no. 6 through classic demographics like "men or women," "professionals or entrepreneurs," etc., according to who you would like to work with = that's your ideal audience

8. From your top 3 strengths, your purpose and your vision, write a one-sentence core brand message; that's for your internal clarity and confidence to know what you stand in the space for and define 3-5 words as your unique brand language

9. From niche, ideal audience and brand message, feel into what type of offers would excite you if you were to work with someone from your soul-aligned audience. Check in the containers (1:1, small or large groups, hybrids), timing (X days, Y weeks, Z months) and online and offline. Start creating 1 to max 3 offers.

This framework and the other elements in the Purpose-Wealth-Cosmos allow you to create your business through you the Light Leader Way.

Next: Enter multidimensional marketing.

You've got your foundation from the above exercise, so it's time to get excited about inviting your aligned audience into your world and your offers. Times of pushy marketing and sales are over, and we are already in the more feminine way of inviting people into our world. Making it multidimensional is the next move as you are multidimensional and likewise, the universe is as well.

What does that mean for marketing?

It is said that it now takes up to 30 touchpoints until someone remembers your brand and you become part of their relevant set of choices to consider when looking for your type of offer. But you don't want to be on social media 24/7, right? Me neither.

That's where multidimensionality comes into play. What you want to create is your unique mix of touchpoints on different platforms where people can experience you and your brand world with their Human Side and their Soul Side. The second part of my SOUL-2SALE framework covers this in detail.

My clients say this blows their mind, and they haven't seen this whole overall approach anywhere in the market yet.

Examples of how you can create touchpoints for the Soul Side of your aligned audience is through sounds, frequencies, art, your soul's native language or just speaking your truth.

Think either reels with light language or light codes, recorded audios including sounds that activate wisdom and the purpose-frequency or NFTs with galactic art. The brain doesn't understand, but this will connect with your audience at soul level.

Or create content speaking truly from your heart and soul in purity. In our loud, fast paced and often superficial world that becomes more and more AI infused, people crave authenticity and connection.

This will give you a shortcut as the 5th dimension marketing connects beyond the surface level straight away.

I've run dozens of clients through this overall process, and they are happily making money doing what they love with soul-aligned clients.

Have a look below to see the eight steps of the Purpose Wealth Cosmos that show the full body of my work.

Purpose-Wealth-Cosmos

Rise into New Earth Success & Soul-Evolution	Create your Multi-Dimensional Business from SOUL2SALE
1 Connecting: Daily Evolution of your Human Side & your Soul Side:	**5 Soul2Sale 1:** (Re)-Birth Your Strengths- & Purpose-Aligned Brand & Business
2 Grounding: Discover your Purpose & Strengths in Action	**6 Self-Expression:** Access the 5th Dimension of Marketing Inside & Share your Message Online
3 New Dimension: Going beyond social media and current platforms	**7 Soul2Sale 2:** Multi-Dimensional Marketing & Sales
4 Expansion: Activate your Psychic Skills & Conscious Evolution	**8 Ascension:** Light Leadership Mastery

MY BIGGER VISION

Let's imagine big for a moment. What could this new earth era look like if we all trusted and created from purpose.

What would it be like if every business owner started with tracing their idea and passion back to their strengths and their purpose-frequency FIRST by identifying exactly their most aligned niche, their most aligned potential clients and brand message to then create offers that feel super exciting for them.

Imagine every business owner creating in a purpose-aligned way impactfully and exactly serving where they are supposed to serve and supporting other people and the world. The level of satisfaction, harmony, creativity, innovation and peace in the world would bring a truly joyful level of wealth, abundance and co-creation.

You wonder what it takes to get there? It takes all of us to step into our power and find our voices, our messages. And our purpose-frequency. It is possible no matter the past experiences if you choose to.

Come with me for a last story of magick that happens when you say yes to purpose:

It's March 1, 2023. I am in London to speak my first international keynote at a trade show. I come to the venue 2hrs before my keynote only to see that my booth I paid for is gone. They say it's a mistake, but there's nothing they can do. I feel the old rage coming up and the well-known sensation of powerlessness. I take a deep breath in and out, letting the emotional wave pass and make a decision: I will not make this mean anything about me or my message.

Minutes later, I am on stage fully on fire with my message "from force into power." I embody what I say. Sixty people listen, nod, and take notes. Jaws drop. Nobody leaves early. I hear applause at the end. People come to me to connect. Fifteen minutes later I make a sale for one of my programs.

It is magick that is available to everyone: connection to purpose-frequency and mastering your human side (emotions, mind, nervous system) and activation of your soul side (soul purpose and wisdom to let it flow).

It didn't happen overnight for me. But if I can do it—an abused and once lost, emotionally numbed, slightly depressed and anxious girl from a German village—you can do it, too. Let me show you how.

You have seen the full journey of how to lead with your purpose-frequency and create new earth business success the joyful way and some insights of my own story of getting there. Now it's your turn. If you asked me, "Judith, what would be the best first step?" My answer would be: "Start connecting with your Human Side and your Soul Side every day for a few minutes to move into more joy, ease, self-mastery and access to your wisdom and gifts"

I have created 4 audio breathing journeys each four minutes long that are fun and easy to integrate every day and that are exactly targeted to support your inner transformation to find your purpose-frequency.

I want to gift them to you, just click here

https://youandjj.ac-page.com/4x4breathingjourneys

I hope you enjoy their power and vibration.

Love & Trust,
Judith

Carmen Cardoso Rocha

Carmen is a Transformational Quantum Coach, VBAC Mentor and Doula helping women across the globe take back their power so that they can achieve their dream births, and live life on their terms! Having breathed and lived through the journey herself she has created the most impactful Coaching Program Birth CEO, because how you birth ultimately defines how you lead!

The Power Within

How You Birth Defines How You Lead

by Carmen Cardoso Rocha

I want to take you back to the beginning... a time where life was simple, where I believed that there was always something within me that felt different to every other person that I knew, but that I always shut down because of fear. It was a time where being perfect wasn't enough and holding myself back from the experiential journey of life meant keeping myself safe. I never felt as my true authentic self; I felt as though I always had to be a certain person to please others, you know that "good little girl," the one that listens the fuck up and does as she's told, the one whose opinion or voice never counted, or meant anything, the one that was consistently shut down from any ideas that would come through... Yes, that one!

I'm sharing this deeply because I want you to know how much this impacted not only my life, but also my first pregnancy and birth, which was an absolute shit show! I was bought up in South Africa by very strict Portuguese parents with a very firm belief that working hard was what called for to achieve financial stability, but that wealth wasn't in the cards for us, that life was dangerous, children needed to be seen and not heard, and that not doing as you are told would bring some serious consequences, I'm talking wooden-spoon consequences... Even the school I attended added fuel to the programming that I already had, as it's your typical entry point onto the conveyor belt system to 'BE' a certain way, 'BIRTH' a certain way, and 'LIVE' life a certain way! Society considers this the average norm, and even with all the layers of conditioning, I kept feeling that there had to be something more to life, but of course, fear and the need to belong kept me chained to just settling and being content with what I had.

As the years went by, my childhood conditioning showed up at every stage in my life with insecurities with myself, imposter syndrome, people pleasing, not being good enough, and thinking before speaking were some of the most predominant ones. I remember taking part in numerous conversations where I would be thinking of what I was going to say each time, but when it came time for me to speak, the conversation had already moved onto something else. This created much doubt in myself, and at many points in my life, it truly broke me.

When I thought I was finally free from the conveyor belt school system, I was thrown right back in to study something that I had no passion for. All I would ever talk about in high school was becoming an actress and going to Hollywood because that was the path I had so deeply wanted to take. Even through all the jokes made, I still continued to hold hope that it was possible… until it wasn't, and my parents completely shut me down. To my parents, acting wasn't a 'proper' job, and even though my Dad had done some of those cowboy comic books way back in the 70s, I was overpowered by their decision, and as the good little girl I was, I put my tail between my legs and succumbed to becoming a glorified beauty therapist, no offense to anyone reading this that is a beauty therapist; if you love what you do, I'm all for it, but for me, this wasn't my choice.

If it's still unclear on how your childhood conditioning can show up in your pregnancy and birth, well I am about to share this with you now… I got pregnant with my first daughter at the age of 32, and I can tell you that I literally did everything by the book, every appointment made I would attend, every test that was recommended I would take, there were no questions asked, and my response to everything was Yes, and even if I didn't want it, I would just soldier on with it. I would also find myself apologising for things that weren't even my fault; as an example, when it came to having my blood taken, if the healthcare provider struggled to find my veins… Yes, I would apologise. As the pregnancy unfolded, I remember receiving a book from a friend that got me thinking about the birth, and my immediate reaction was thinking to myself 'Fuck! How the hell am I going to get this baby out?' and then I closed the book and never looked at it again. I decided that not thinking about my number one birth fear would make it go away, but unfortunately it didn't. As my estimated due date approached, (yes, I, too, have held onto that ridiculous mathematical calculation that makes no freaking sense at all, especially when you realise that for approximately two of those weeks, you aren't even pregnant) my midwife appointments became more frequent. She would palpate my bump to check the baby's position, and at every appointment, she would say that the baby was head down. I never blinked, or questioned even though every fibre in my being felt that this wasn't right. As the birthing day arrived, guess what happened? It turned out my baby girl was breech, she had never been head down to begin with, she had always been in a seated position. Of course, healthcare providers provided me with two options, I could either have a caesarean, or I could birth her vaginally, however there wasn't anyone skilled enough to facilitate a breech birth. Add a layer of deep fear on top of this, and voila, caesarean birth it was, but this surgical procedure wouldn't be happening yet; I would need to wait for my turn in a ward, without my husband, whilst labouring, which takes cruelty to a whole other level! Can you guess what my response was to that?!

After four hours of being attached to the hospital bed by monitors, whilst experiencing every single contraction unsupported and alone, they were finally ready for me. My husband had a 30-minute window to get back to the hospital; we were prepped and ready to go! My baby girl was born, and whilst I was happy that she was here, part of me kept thinking, "Why me?" Why have so many others achieved their natural birth, why was my baby girl cut out of me, I felt so much guilt and shame of the outcome for years later until I realised that it was fear, and my childhood conditioning that was the culprit behind how I was leading in birth, in my business and in my life!

Two babies and a miscarriage later, I found myself entering a new world… a world of deep inner self discovery and healing, a world where peeling back each onion layer bought me closer to another realisation of just how small we have been playing all this time. I began to understand that I didn't know who I really was at a deep core level because I had carried so much from everyone else. I was holding onto their shit, their beliefs, their fears… I recall in my younger years my higher self always coming up to lead with love and trust, but then my ego gripping onto me like it truly owned me, was more than willing me to play it safe and stay small. It's taken some time to move past the discomfort, to heal, and to realise that true change goes way deeper than just the power of the mind, it really starts at a much deeper cellular level!

My healing journey has opened so much, it's given me access to a part of my mind that I wasn't able to fully connect with, where divine downloads do happen. The thing is that I am no different from you, or anyone else, we can all connect with this innate power, it's within us, and it's always been there; however, for most of us, it's been consistently shut down by all the external noise. Do you remember a time when you used to daydream? Then some ball-breaker came along and told you to snap out of it? That was your higher self, exploring a variety of infinite possibilities, the ball-breaker, well, I'm sure you will be able to figure out who that was…. It might've even been the same person that killed the belief that Santa Claus isn't real! I really want you to read my next few words carefully… Ignore all the crap that you've ever heard about getting your head out of the clouds, I encourage you to keep your head as high up in the clouds as possible so that you can call in your dream vision, be it your birth, your business, or your life. If you can visualise it and feel it, it means that it's already happening in the metaphysical world, keep holding the vision and lead from a place of certainty that it is already yours.

I want to share a bit about my journey with visualising. Soon after my miscarriage, I found myself going through a 6-month spiral of negative pregnancy tests, every month bought newfound hope, which was then completely shattered. I realise now that I was chasing the pregnancy, and that's exactly why it wasn't showing up. It wasn't until I attended a Tony Robbins event where everything shifted, we did this powerful exercise that included visualisation, and in my vision, I saw myself pregnant, then going onto achieve my VBA2C (vaginal birth after 2 caesareans), it felt so real that I had tears of joy in my eyes. I was in such a calm place, and that was the first time in months that I was able to fully surrender knowing that it would all work out. Ten days later I got my positive pregnancy test… the main reason for me was because I fell into trust, and I was able to fully let go! When we can get to a place of trust and surrender, that's where the true magic happens! The main reason is because you have met your co-creator halfway, and now this is where they come to deliver your manifestation in the most unexpected way! I want you to remember that everything that you are manifesting right now is a co-creation between you and the Universe. You have created the vision that you desire, you have taken the inspired action from a place of higher self, and now the hardest part of all is surrendering to the Universe and trusting that your manifestation is on its way.

Surrendering and trusting is so hard and uncomfortable for so many of us, I know because I have been there, and even now and then the struggle to fully trust and let go still shows up. There is a difference though, and this is something I want you to take away from this chapter. I invite you to ask yourself questions every time the need to control comes through. Get curious about why you are struggling to let go and why you feel the need to control the outcome? One of my coaches asked me at one point in time whether I was a control freak? Of course, I was shocked, and straight away denied it because I was in complete denial; I was doing just that, trying to control the outcome! So, I want you to ponder the question: Am I a control freak? This will give you an opportunity to discover any patterns that keep showing up, so that you can learn from them. I am a big believer that patterns are showing up in life to teach us that there is another way.

Let me give you a business example, have you ever been in a position where you have been chasing the clients, the money, and as you are freaking out about the payments you have coming out, and barely any money to your name… what shows up?... Crickets! Nada! Nothing! Want to know why? You are in lack, and trying to control the outcome, which is only putting you in a worse position!

How about a time where you fully let go of the outcome, and you were having fun, what happened then? Clients showed up or payments were made right? This happened because you were in flow! I have found the same thing happening in birth where you get to manifest the good stuff and the bad stuff, and I want to share another example with you. In 2021, I was pregnant with my daughter, Luna, and going in for my 20-week scan when they discovered that my placenta was covering my cervix quite a bit, and they also believed that my placenta was attached to my uterine scar, and if that was the case, well then, let's just say that I could kiss my VBA2C goodbye. Now, I could've chosen to give up, but I left that appointment affirming that my placenta would be sitting up high, and that my uterine scar wasn't going to be a problem. I went on this internal rant from the minute I left the appointment right up until I sat down in my car where I affirmed that it was done, and that I no longer needed to think about it. A few weeks later I went into another appointment to check my placenta, and it was sitting up high which was no surprise to me, but when I asked the sonographer about my uterine scar, she asked, "What scar?" She couldn't see anything! I just want to add that she did both an external and internal scan at my 32-week appointment! Make no mistake that you get to call in the good and the bad, I have had clients preparing for a set type of birth, only to manifest the complete opposite based on what they were most fearing at the time. You can consciously choose to affirm that all was well; however, on a subconscious level, the stored trauma that hasn't been healed will tell a completely different story. I have also seen clients' births unfold based on stories that they have heard from friends, family, and social media.

It's not necessarily the story as such, but it's the energetic feelings that you experience and hold onto whilst you are listening in, and that alone has the powerful ability to call it in! I do want to say that when you can achieve your utopian birth like I and so many of my clients have, you are left with an overwhelming sense of achievement that you can truly move mountains and accomplish anything that your heart desires!

You are Superhuman with incredible powers! Did you realise that? I want you to stop reading for a minute, put on your favourite dance song and celebrate just how freaking amazing and powerful your body is! It has the power to merge a sperm and egg to create human life, it has the power to create a supporting organ, aka the placenta, that nourishes your growing baby; if that's not powerful, then I have no idea what is! So why do we spend so much time underestimating how powerful we truly are, not only when it comes to birth, but in our business and in life too? It's everything that we are holding onto from past generational trauma, societal conditioning, and the patriarchy. I recall being a little girl where women couldn't show power, positions of power were taken on by men, being a homemaker was the primary role of a woman, and that we needed to be "good girls." Of course, my mother was one of the people that broke the pattern of being a homemaker, because she was self-employed and the main bread winner for our family, however that came at the cost of working hard and sacrificing so much. I invite you to start exploring your family lineage, how the women in your family birthed, any traumas they experienced, and what their main beliefs were about life in general and themselves. This will give you an amazing place to begin understanding what could be stored within you on a cellular level because the body will keep the score of everything that has ever happened in your life so far, as well as any traumas that have occurred in past generations. Your main responsibility will be to heal from this, so that you can create safety within your body.

This brings me to an important piece of the puzzle, your psoas muscle. Listen up because this is one of the most important muscles that you are going to need to nurture! The psoas muscle aka the muscle of the soul, is deeply connected to birth and leadership because it holds our trauma and is primarily responsible for our fight/flight/freeze/fawn/flop response. If you haven't had the opportunity to work through the trauma, be it big or small, and you haven't had the opportunity to create safety within your body, then this muscle will be on consistent high alert! This can show up in a variety of ways, lower back, hip, or groin pain, painful intercourse, postural problems, decreased bowel movements, chest breathing, and feeling exhausted to name a few. Having a healthy psoas muscle that is soft and released is essential in birth because when the psoas is in an optimal state, it creates a spiralling motion to help baby navigate further down into the pelvis. A released psoas can determine how easily our pelvis opens in birth, which creates an optimal environment for baby's arrival earthside. Oh, and did I mention, our pelvis is our financial seat of abundance! So, you might be wondering right now how you would do this? I'm going to share the three main things that I found helpful to create safety in my psoas muscle:

1. **WORKING THROUGH MY PREVIOUS BIRTH AND CHILD-HOOD TRAUMAS** — this was one of the biggest steps in creating safety in my body. When I was able to heal from past experiences, I was able to look at my third daughter's birthing journey through a different lens, which also impacted how I was able to lead in my business.

2. **CONSTRUCTIVE REST POSE** — this is one of my most favourite poses when it comes to softening your psoas muscle because it really gives you the opportunity to stop and just be. There were so many insights that came through from just being in this position. If you are unsure what this pose is, there is a gift at the end of my chapter, and I will share how you can find out more about this resting pose.

3. **REGULATING MY NERVOUS SYSTEM** — If I can create a space where I feel regulated, calm and at peace, I am then able to navigate through birth, business and life without my psoas being triggered by the rush of adrenaline.

There are a number of other ways to create a healthy psoas, and this is something that I always explore within my client sessions because it is important to me that they can lead from a deeper place of knowing that their utopian birth, business and life is just on the other side of the discomfort. If we can help create an optimal environment for our psoas, then I can promise you that moving through the discomfort to where growth happens will be an easier journey to ride out.

Please know that all probabilities in life, business and birth are possible if you have visualised them, then it's already in the Quantum Realm, but the number one thing that will get in the way of us achieving the life, the business, and the birth that we want will be our current identity. Of course, we want it all; however, when we are thrown into the depths of the discomfort, it's our identity along with all of the bullshit that we have been telling ourselves for all of our life that wins! Someone that holds the identity that they are a good girl, afraid to take big bold steps, unlucky, not good at making decisions, hardworking, and impatient will never achieve a utopian birth, let alone a successful business. I know this because I was that person! For me to get to where I am today, I needed to shed my old identity, I needed to embody the version of myself that had already achieved the dream birth, business, and life. I then had to take inspired action from the version of the person that had already achieved all those things. This was one of the hardest parts especially because I was someone that has been bought up to believe that working hard was the only way to go, which is a very masculine energy trait! Some action is required, however not the way that I was doing things, which almost led me to a full burnout on several occasions.

Inspired action feels different than regular 'get your arse to work' action, it's a pull rather than a push, it brings up excitement rather than dread, and you feel in flow rather than stagnant. Hopefully with this brief explanation, you will start distinguishing the difference when acting from a soul-aligned place. Creation requires a level of both masculine and feminine energy, as you have learned above. The masculine energy is all about the doing; however, when manifesting this, it isn't from a place of hustle, but rather from a place of flow. Once you have put in the aligned-inspired action, now comes the hardest part of all that so many people struggle with: Leaning into trust and surrendering which is very much a feminine energy trait! The number one reason why this is so hard is because we love to control things. Remember the control freak conversation earlier in this chapter? You can honestly thank the control freak within you because they are one of the main reasons why your manifestations aren't becoming part of your reality!

I want you to spend some time reflecting on the following: Imagine you had already achieved the utopian birth, business and life, would you be questioning where or how it was coming?

No, you wouldn't because you would've already achieved it! So why do we still try and control things? It's your software that's faulty, and it just simply needs a full reboot! In fact, until you can start to give your subconscious mind evidence that things are working out for you, it can be somewhat hard to fully trust and let go. I've had to learn this the hard way. A previous coach I worked with a few years ago helped me price a high-ticket offering at a certain level that I believed was fully out of my comfort zone, the result was a complete mental and emotional shut down, no sales, and me hitting rock bottom. This resulted in me getting a temp job to make ends meet, being again in hustle mode and completely out of alignment. It wasn't until I began to realise with the help of my new coach that there was a part of me that needed to be healed, my Mother and Father wound ran deep, and this is why I didn't feel worthy of charging the higher price point. When I was able to work through the things that were coming up, I also noticed more clients flowing in and paying the prices that aligned to where I was on my journey, even though those price points still felt uncomfortable. I was finally able to give my subconscious mind the proof it needed, that clients were buying my higher priced offering, and this then moved me to increase my pricing to the next level of discomfort. This new-found knowledge/confidence has also helped me further trust and surrender! I've been using a number of methods with my clients to help lead them in their birth, business, and life, and it's totally working for them!

You might be wondering how birth fits into surrendering and trusting… well, why wouldn't it? If there was ever a time in a woman's life that she would need to lean into letting go, it would totally be during birth. I recall being in labour with my daughter Luna, and an obstacle being thrown at me. You know the usual time restraints that healthcare providers love putting on birth, especially when many of us know that birth isn't a simple textbook process. I needed to be transferred to the labour ward because, God-forbid, my labour was "taking too long!" The pressure to transfer was so intense, and at one point, it honestly felt as though I was in a CIA black site being tortured until they were able to break me (of course I've only ever witnessed this in the movies). Like any regular person, I resisted as much as I possibly could, but then decided hours later that I would go because I needed to sleep otherwise this birth wasn't going to work. I remember being transferred through to the labour ward as I was kneeling on a wheelchair, and as I gripped onto the chair through each surge, the voice inside my head started. "It's game over! You are going up to the labour ward, you will end up with another c-section! Think of all the people you are letting down, yourself included!" This went on for about a minute, then I consciously jumped in and told my subconscious mind to quiet the fuck down! It wasn't game over! I was just getting started and needed to sleep so that I could regain my strength and smash my birth! So that's exactly what I did, but that only happened because I was able to fully let go, and I had a deep knowing that everything was going to work out as it divinely needed to. Later that day I found out the real reason why they wanted to transfer me; it was because the Birth Centre was closed due to staff shortages, so, talk about trying to derail a perfectly normal birth? Yup, it's seriously messed up, and the worst part is that this happens way too often! When fear is riding shotgun, you will never be in a place where you can fully let go; you need to work through what's going on in your internal world first.

As I mentioned my birth was the most utopia moment in my life. I honestly couldn't believe that I had done it. I wanted to shout it out to the world, let everyone know that they can achieve their dream birth outcome… and I did just that! By the time my baby girl was two weeks old, I began coaching my birth clients online, my daughter would be either sleeping or feeding on me, and it really worked beautifully. Even now that she's a bit older, she will still be part of some sessions, and she usually falls asleep as I get started. I guess my voice is either boring her to sleep or soothing her to sleep. I prefer the latter. When I say that you can literally create anything, this is truly a possibility, I have seen my life pivot in the most mysterious ways since beginning this deeper level work, the one thing that has always stood out is the identity that I have chosen to embody. I am no longer that perfect, good girl that colours in the lines and works on pleasing every soul on this planet. I let that shit go a long time ago!

So many women feel that they need to choose between being a parent and running their own business, but what if you could do both? A few years ago, this had always been my initial thought that the two couldn't co-exist, that it would seem unprofessional, and how could it even be possible? Guess I proved the old version of myself wrong again! It is totally possible! The first step is letting people know that you and your baby come as a package, and that it's a non-negotiable, already there you are asking the universe to send you aligned clients that understand and are okay with how you lead in your business. The next step is to be open with your clients, that you are caring for a newborn and that sometimes unexpected things can happen. I'll give you an example. Luna was about three months old, and I was coaching a client about the trauma she had experienced in her first birth, then suddenly, Luna had the biggest poonami ever! For those of you that don't know what that is, I'll explain, it's the biggest shit storm that no nappy could ever withstand. I mean it went all the way up her little back! So, here is what I did, I told my client what had happened, and that I needed to change her. We both giggled, and then continued our conversation as I changed Luna. This created normality for my client and gave her evidence that it's okay, and that she could lead her business in the same way if she wanted to. My client is coaching women together with her baby now!

One thing I want you to realise is that if you have found your purpose, you truly love what you do, and you lead from a place of trust, then it will always work out for you, and for the greater good of all.

Wherever you are on your journey right now, I want you to believe that parenting your newborn and entrepreneurship can totally co-exist! If you are ready to call it in, I want you to begin visualising what your utopia birth, business and life looks like to you. Once you have done that, you are going to get clear on the identity of the person that already has it all, and lead from that very place! Leading from your new identity even if everything around you feels hard can be tricky, and this is why never losing sight of our vision is everything! Remember your subconscious mind doesn't know the difference between what is real and what is imagined, so the clearer you can get with your vision the better. As my coach says, the universe will then provide you with the breadcrumbs necessary so that you can begin to take the inspired action to call in everything your heart desires and feel financially supported during your Forth trimester.

If you are ready to call in your dream birth, business and life, then I want you to go right ahead and download this free gift below because it is truly time to Unleash Your Superpowers!

Free Visualisation and Workbook:

https://thequantumbirthdoula.podia.com/utopia-breath-work-meditation

Deanna Vicera

Reverend Deanna L. Vicera (Dr.D)- Psychic, received messages from the other side at a young age, developing with this knowing and clairaudience through adulthood. Later, going through a spiritual awakening she gravitated to spiritual counseling, and meditation, pursued certifications as a Reiki Master, life coach (IPEC), psychic medium, intuitive consultant (HSI), and ordained spiritualist minister.

If We Truly Remembered Our Soul's Purpose, Would We Choose to Live Differently?

by Deanna Vicera

"If we truly remembered our soul's purpose, would we choose to live differently?"

Have you ever stood at the ocean's shoreline looking out into the ocean just like the conscious collective … and asked yourself these questions?

* Have you ever experienced déjà vu? A knowing?

* Have you ever heard voices in your head?

* What if there really were no coincidences, and what is all of this?

* What if it was really a soul's recollection of what your purpose was here on earth before we incarnated?

* What if we wrote our life's purpose, and what if the story here on earth was really a dream and all for the purpose of soul evolution?

* What does it mean to wake up from this dream?

* What is a soul? Does the soul have a mind?

- What is your ego? The who of who you truly are, your true authentic self, and do you have a purpose?

- We truly come into this world with nothing, and we exit with nothing. How can that be?

- What is all of this? What is my soul's true purpose?

As a young child, looking out into the vast sea of possibilities, I sat in the sand as the waves rolled in reflecting the sunlight off their white caps, feeling the crisp ocean breeze blow through my hair, smelling the salt air, hearing the sound of the gulls harmonize in sync creating a peaceful and surreal experience at the water's edge …. I asked myself those questions.

As the cold water rushed in, a crashing sound of the waves hitting the ocean floor mixed with the sand between my fingers and toes.

I remember my eyes opened wide looking out in amazement far beyond what the eyes could see at an entire ocean as if it were the collective before me and as if my body were a container holding a cup of the ocean representing Spirit, which then individually was colored creating each unique soul. What was this? What was I re-membering? It was almost as if I held a key to unlocking the truths of discovering a secret to this lifetime.

Could this just be the beginning of explaining the soul?

What is the soul if not our true authentic self.

The soul is the "I am" of who we truly are. The soul is the true spiritual essence of one's being including personality, identity, and memories that has been proven to ascend death by persons that have had near-death experiences, and/or by evidential medi-umship, including, but not limited to communication with those souls that have crossed over.

What is ego? It's the false sense of self.

From an esoteric point of view and spiritually speaking, ego is the false sense of self, which prohibits us from having a universal or collective existence. It is what causes separation from other beings, the universe and the higher power.

A soul is all loving and pure that gets buried in the darkness of the ego's hurt, pain, and brokenness. A soul shines from time to time when the ego is not overshadowing and in the forefront.

The ego is a powerful one for it causes the soul to retreat, holds onto false beliefs, and continues to hold the soul hostage in its made-up world.

What if we continue to allow the ego to operate through us and the soul stayed locked away? We would miss out on living. We would miss out on shining. We would miss out on showing up as our true authentic self.

We would miss out on opportunities in our path including growth.

Is it worth it?

Who needs to heal? Who is hurt? Who is overwhelmed?

Who is all loving?

Who is showing up?

The ego that needs to put on a show or the true essence of who you are as we drop the ego and shine full of wisdom and knowledge?

Reflections are our best teachers, and love is our best healer. The choice is yours.

Keep showing up the Who of who you truly are and allow the ego to die and you will find yourself—the all-loving soul, a soul that can soar to new heights, take on the world, and become more than you ever imagined!

It is already written, so continue to step out of this fairy tale (or nightmare) and into your dreams and desires… your true reality.

EGO is the False Self. The Soul is the True Self.

THE EGO		THE SOUL
False Self		True self
Me		We
Separation		Unity
Blame		Understanding
Hostility		Friendliness
Resentment		Forgiveness
Pride		Love
Complain		Gratitude
Jealousy		Co-Happiness
Anger		Joy
Power	VS.	Humble
Materialism		Spiritualism
Madness		Wisdom
War		Peace
Coldness		Sympathy
Past/ future		NOW
Intolerance		Tolerance
Egoism		Altruism
Self Denial		Self-Acceptance
Wanting Everything		Simplicity
Doing		Being

What are the contracts on the other side?

A belief that before every incarnation lifetime after lifetime our chosen soul family creates written contracts between our souls on the other side or what some call the fifth dimension and/or heaven. These contracts contain the actions of others and the roles they play here on earth, to recreate the pains of the past for soul evolution carrying out the contracts from long ago.

These contracts were written from love, yet deliver such pain. The remembering … The human experience that is occurring for only one purpose, which is soul evolution. Is life really happening? What is this? This is just a dream of a play where the script was written by us for us long ago on the other side.

The players, the characters, the lead role and the supporting actors… we are all just a part of the divine plan.

It is the level of consciousness from how and where we are viewing this amphitheater called life. Are we gifted enough to see behind the veil? Do you remember long ago when we were standing before the higher power writing our script?

Or are we led around by our mind, riding the rollercoaster of the ups and downs of life? Do we show up as our true authentic self, which is the sole reason we are here for evolution? Or is our ego the powerful master or so we think, which allows it to tell us lies of what we need or who we are or what will even make us happy in the moment.

How many times can we not stand in our truths just to feel pain and disappointment because the mind, our ego, lead us astray.

When is it time to quiet the mind and look within and allow our inner knowing to lead in trust, faith, and acceptance of the divine plan?

When do we stop asking why this is happening and look deeper into remembering?

Remembering not only why this is happening in this pre-orchestrated play of life but truly remembering its purpose.

Depending on the lens through which we view life, we can usually have a greater knowing that what is happening in every moment is for the greater good. We can usually remember at this level of consciousness that people, places, and things were put forth in our life the way it was written. Then, we go one step further and find forgiveness in our human form for whatever is occurring at the moment and true acceptance that it is for our greater good.

The last phase is to remember why we had a contract and a plan for these events to occur.

When we look deep within, everything happens in divine timing for our own healing and our souls to ascend upward and evolve. Does any of this make analytical sense? Yes, in the intellectual mind, being the light unto others, and by sharing a piece of the journey for self-introspection. We all agree that in order to heal we must feel pain. Through pain comes growth! And we will repeat the lesson and keep getting the lesson until we learn the lesson. It will usually come in the hardest form if we do not learn the lesson the first time around, lifetime after lifetime. Our minds and ego can be very stubborn! So, as we quiet the mind and come from our soul, we are ascending upward in soul evolution to achieve the highest form and not return to the dream we call life.

What does life here on earth look like as we know it from the human perspective?

We see the human struggle of grief, betrayal, love, fear, addiction, change and death to name a few.

We are going to examine each of these human struggles one by one and see how the egoic mind may react to them. Let's see how the ego deals with them, and let's see what that looks like in the human experience.

The ego versus the soul's perspective:

WHAT IS GRIEF? Grief is a deep feeling of sorrow. How do we handle grief in everyday life?

We all handle grief differently depending on the lens at which we are looking through in the moment and as we are looking through the lens, is it the soul's or ego's perspective? This also is dependent on the level of one's conscious awareness.

Grief could be caused by the loss of something or someone during the course of this journey.

Grief causes waves of feelings and emotions which in turn cause acceptance and resistance depending on if it is the egoic mind, which are the stories in our head, versus the soul which represents our true authentic self that believes life is eternal and everything has already been written for us by us on the other side.

It is the internal war and the battle within.

It is the difference between how could all this have happened to me, as opposed to the universe has a plan, and I am grateful for this to happen now so that I may grow, evolve and change to accept the unfolding of a beautiful journey that lies ahead that I cannot see just yet. It is the difference between being stuck and accepting we are here for nothing more than soul evolution.

The universe always has a way to hand us an element of surprise when we least expect it. We always feel like we are not ready, but the higher power knows better and best. What we resist persists. I am speaking from experience. The tears that flow, the pain from within. Where does it all come from? Grief? Or is it truly attachment? Being attached to the stories in our mind or our ego. What we thought life should be as opposed to what is.

How can we not trust the universe when it has led to the unfolding of a grand plan before us? We have seen the unforeseen in miraculous ways. How did we get here? Life unfolded. What are we truly remembering? Is this real? Or are we just waking up?

Yet, moving forward in life our mind is full of self-doubt. Where is our faith? Where is our trust in divine timing? We have that true inner knowing. If we would only spend as much time listening to that as we do the stories in our head. No one said this was easy. But as we keep looking within and uncovering the place our pain originated from that keeps us stuck in grief and we heal, we continue to ascend upward looking outward and within from a completely new perspective and level of consciousness in truth, faith and trust. We become lighter. We flow with the law of attraction and align with like energy. We live in gratitude and acceptance as the waves of life keep the fire lit and outwardly glow in radiance once again. It helps us step into our power, hold our ground and make decisions from love and truth with our free will. We start to trust our knowing!

Everything is for me, and the universe has a plan! So, if life is eternal and it is already written, then is grief real? Or are we truly just holding onto form? Acceptance is huge, and it allows us to become unstuck from this attachment we call grief.

Trust it, says the soul.

FEAR

WHAT IS FEAR? An unpleasant and often strong emotion caused by expectation or awareness of danger or worry.

FEAR is

> *False Evidence Appearing Real.*
> *Fear Everything And Run,* says the ego.

How does fear affect us in everyday life?

How do we live our best life when fear presents itself? With intuition and awareness says the soul.

The only thing that keeps us stuck in fear and from moving on is our ego. It's not anyone or any circumstance. It is the story we create in the mind.

Ego says fear is real. However, when we stop the story, the pain subsides, and we grow and evolve.

Spirit or your soul says fear is an illusion that we created in the mind to use as a "proceed with caution," yet ego holds it in the highest regard as truth in every moment yet the soul says look within at the moment and there is nothing to fear.

Our mind can continue blaming others and the circumstances or we can make the conscious decision to move forward in TRUST, which is the polar opposite of fear.

TRUST IS TOTALLY RELYING UPON SPIRITUAL TRUTH!

All the answers lie within and have absolutely nothing to do with anyone but you! Try listening to your higher self and miracles do happen. Life unfolds beyond your wildest dreams.

Face Everything And Rise says the soul.

LOVE

WHAT IS LOVE? Love is an intense feeling and attraction to something or another being with acceptance and without conditions.

Is loving more actually letting go?

How are we affected by this?

Is love eternal?

What is ego versus true love?

What is unconditional love?

Loving someone truly, deeply from our soul means without ever having any conditions. Loving someone without conditions means so much, yet so little to the ego. When we truly love someone from our soul, they are free, which in turn is only a reflection of our very own self.

Hence, love is only a reflection of You, self-love.

One could recognize Ego love vs. true spiritual love.

Two totally different kinds of love are dependent upon the level of consciousness two people are operating from on their journey. Have you ever recognized what some people label a toxic relationship? Without judgement, I simply say it's a relationship that doesn't resonate with me today. Just a different level of consciousness. Some relationships exist with control, lies, deceit, cheating, betrayal, conflict, arguments, gaslighting, and manipulation, just to name a few and this is their "love." "But I love you" is ego love.

Love is a verb—given one life—a soul that is here to evolve and be free!

A life of freedom … to be love … to have self-love is purest in form where one can reflect that very love back with another connected soul.

True spiritual love—how do we attain such love?

Our journey here is independent of other's reactions, behaviors, emotions, thoughts, etc. We simply love from the very love we show and give to ourselves and the very love that we are no matter what is going on around us. When we love ourselves completely, we will make other choices for ourselves out of love instead of from the ego which most of the time is fear.

When we truly are waking up and walk through enough pain, we will become love, reflect and desire true love and choose to be the very love we ourselves want, we will then reflect back from those around us at all cost, others will fade away and we will choose differently as they will no longer serve our soul.

Have you ever connected with someone's soul in the moment only to wonder who that person was in the next moment?

The very Ego true self-split!

Depending on your lens, one can recognize someone's soul (the love that they are) and watch them still operate from their mind (the ego), which just hasn't learned to be quiet, take the back seat and hence how I refer to it as "needing to die." It's truly recognizable and amazing to see what one can reflect back in love.

So, keep loving oneself. Keep being the love that you were born to be.

And cherish the moments that very love is reflected back with another soul because it is truly an amazing experience.

And always remember—goodbyes are not forever.

When two people are connected in love deep within their soul, oftentimes there are human lessons and karma that must play out in the dance of life. A part of love is actually letting go for the souls to evolve and grow. A hard decision along the journey is to love without conditions, honor one another without feeding the ego and avoid the pains of the past currently in the present by forcing yourself to feel that pain and do the hard work so one can have clarity and stop allowing the ego to be fed and hold on.

Avoidance is sneaky but recognizable. What do we do to avoid the pain? We run. We keep busy. We hide. Hide from our own shadows. "It's love" says the ego.

"Oh, contraire," says the soul.

Love does not cause pain. Love is a mere reflection of oneself and until the soul can step forward without the shadow of the ego, it is not free, whole, or authentic and causes pain and destruction to itself and anyone in its path; for as the soul connects, the ego destroys. It is one's awareness to see one's own true self and the ego split. What is your shadow, and why is it lurking? What is it destroying? Is it the inner child holding on? A child in pain afraid to be left yet again? Is it the imprints of our parental dynamics that we remember from so long ago, yet cannot face? Is it the co-dependent connection that was implanted within the ego that we replay and have become? Is it the child's fear of not being good enough? A journey already taken and cast behind in a family dynamic?

How free are we? How free can we be? It only takes doing the work, looking within and letting go because on the other side of this darkness is a light that shines and illuminates that very soul without the ego's shadow.

It's that soul connection that stands in truth but must stand alone. The only way through it is to heal the pain and allow the ego to fade away and die! A hard ask? A simple feat like a moth to a flame; it only takes the courage and the strength to look within and choose living over dying, agony over defeat, life over going through the motions. A true spiritual love versus. ego love. The path is yours.

Time is always but an illusion yet waits for no one, so why do we continue to waste another second of it? Our egos feel entitled, yet death can steal the soul. Choose life. Choose love and start remembering.

BETRAYAL

WHAT IS BETRAYAL? Betrayal is going against or breaking one's core values such as one's trust or moral or ethical standards.

Betrayal can cut our ego's self to the core, but does betrayal exist at the soul level?

Betrayal seems as if it is done to you says the ego. We create a whole story in our head of what another being set out to do in the moment to us. Yet on the soul level, the other being was inadvertently just living in the moment and doing their best on their journey dependent on what level of consciousness they were living and what part of the who that they truly are is stepping forward, in other words, who was stepping forward? Was it their ego or their true authentic self, their soul?

ADDICTION

WHAT IS ADDICTION? A chronic condition such as substance abuse or a negative behavior that one loses control over.

Why do we want it? Are we filling a void? Are we satisfying a feeling?

It is all a part of the ego's wants and desires. The soul needs nothing.

The ego's wants and desires become an overwhelming feeling from the pains of the past. These feelings that arise deep within oneself cause the egoic mind to start to chatter. The ego's identity steps forward in control, creating stories in our head that now become reality. Our new-found reality stirs up emotions in us and we then act out in our chosen addictive behavior trying to fill the void of the very feeling that started the addiction cycle.

The all-loving soul, when at a high level of consciousness, need not fill any such feeling within. The soul wants for nothing but its mere existence without judgment in gratitude of love, acceptance and truth of what is.

CHANGE

WHAT DOES IT MEAN TO TRULY CHANGE? What or who am I changing?

What I discovered while working with human nature, is that we are all hoarders (to different degrees) of our concepts and experiences within our very own egoic mind.

Even if people suffocate us, keep us in filth and cramp our comfort to move freely, or go against our most sacred values, we do not make a different choice, instead we cling to them because they are our mind's precious possessions!

To everyone else, they can be toxic, but not to us. That is why people are not willing to change. People change when they have clarity from a different conscious awareness, and they are called upon by a higher power to truly be free and when they allow grace to enter no longer live in their own ego identity.

That is the very reason the true self is all loving, and perfect spiritual love casts out all fear by the grace of God.

Sometimes all we can do is pray for those who come from a negative energy of manipulation and control because to them it's just a "win." It's the egoic mind.

There's never any spiritual love coming from their soul.

No one changes without doing the work. And the work is years of undoing old patterns of the past including the thoughts in our head because we buy into deception with our minds.

And everything we thought no longer exists, so what was our life all about?

We can't possibly judge it as a lie. We cannot rationalize or analyze this. All we can do is accept life in cycles. As we grow, cycles end for our higher good, and a new cycle begins.

The universe brings us our intended path on a higher level of consciousness.

Search for the truth.

Although sometimes we allow our minds to get stuck instead of listening to our soul, life is not hard. We choose to make it that way with stories in our head. But in the end, as we wake up from the ego's dream, we always remember that the soul knows.

DEATH

HOW DO WE HANDLE DEATH HERE ON EARTH? How does our ego handle it versus our soul? What is death as the human form knows it to be? Death is a person or animal that has passed on in human form as we know it. Life is eternal. The soul transitions and ascends upward lifetime after lifetime. It's the body or human vessel that dies along with the ego.

The ego grieves death as a loss. The longing or missing from that human form and attachment. The soul knows no separation. We are all one.

The child ever-so innocent sitting on the water's edge truly remembering their soul's purpose, the contracts on the other side, the reason we incarnated into this dream state, and now the awakening. Waking up to our true authentic self and realizing what life's struggles were really all about. Realizing we are all allowed to stay asleep in the unconscious mind and continue to want for different—every step of the journey and suffer, or we can accept it.

Everything happening here on earth was just the classroom done for us and by us in creating the contracts with our soul family on the other side before we incarnated in this lifetime for the evolution of our soul. We are here for soul evolution and later ascend upward closer to the state of transition and human death when our lessons are learned and/or the contracts are fulfilled.

Yes, we were also given what is called free will along the journey. Free will is the decision whether conscious or unconscious made to take us down different paths in this lifetime depending on how the soul is proceeding with the evolution set forth before them.

So, ask yourself, if you truly remembered why your soul came to earth, would you choose to live life differently?

Would you choose a new sense of freedom in this lifetime? To be free of the ego, to wake up from this dream we call life and truly realize we are all a part of a bigger plan, the collective consciousness.

Would we judge others holding resentment in our mind's judgment of what is being done to us in everyday life?

Or would we truly accept that all of this was part of remembering the divine plan and allowing life to unfold with curiosity and excitement and to smile and laugh at the hard lessons we chose for ourselves because we all believe that the who of who I am is a worthy, unique individual soul that contributes to the conscious collective as a whole of raising the vibration of humanity and waking up to all the love that we were born with more wisdom, knowledge and acceptance for what is in every moment and those we are here to assist with their contracts and shine light upon in love.

This is the journey. Do we choose to awaken and live free in every moment to take the next step?

Our mind says look at what is being done to me!

Our soul says look at what is happening and how it is bringing us a reflection, a lesson, or the why this is happening in the 3D (earth) for the 5D (soul) and its purpose on the journey! To grow, to evolve, to return to LOVE.

Oneness and wholeness as we ascend upward. It is truly an amazing journey!

Do we dare to remember?

To connect with me further, I invite you to join my Facebook page, Messages from the Skyye:

https://www.facebook.com/DivinenReborn

Joanne Webb

Loving Warrior Goddess Joanne Webb (The Happiness Hustler), a mum of 4, visionary, lightworker, Self-Love expert, and Quantum Coach, is changing the world with Conscious Love.

Jo awakens her clients and propels them into abundance, thriving, passionate, excited for life, feeling unconditionally loved, with confidence to create the life of their dreams and their biggest successes.

Changing the World with LOVE

by Joanne Webb

Dear Reader,

As you are here, I know you are a Lightworker with unique gifts, talents and insights to offer the world. Now more than ever, the world needs you to step up and let your light shine. This chapter has three parts that intermingle along life's journey; these are not steps but components to help individuals step into their unique superpowers.

LOVE THY SELF

The night I chose Love, he hit, throttled, straddled, and slapped me repeatedly. I fought, kicked, bit and wriggled my way free.

My biggest lesson? Love is always the answer.

But what is Love? It's not all just fairytales and romantic (although I do love all that too). No, Love is a choice, a way of living, a filter. Love is **ENERGY**. And right now, this world, this beautiful planet, needs more Love than ever before. So, I invite you to join me as a Pioneer of the Conscious Love Revolution.

In a room of dark, when one light shines, it changes the room. It makes a difference and can be seen by all. The same cannot be said for the reverse. So, please don't ever underestimate what little 'ole you can do in the world if you choose Love and Lead with Light. It will change your life and the lives of everyone you encounter.

To be Love, spread Love, and live from Conscious Love, it starts with self.

The night I chose Love, he hit, throttled, straddled, and slapped me repeatedly. I fought, kicked, bit and wriggled my way free.

That wasn't the worst of it, though. The hours of sneering nasty remarks in my face and bullying me while cornered in the kitchen were low. But then he spat at me. Right in my face. Not once or even twice, but three times. It was disgusting and sickening to the core.

And all this because a girlfriend who was moving back to the UK had popped over for dinner, and I'd had given her my attention, maybe laughed a few times and had a pleasant evening.

After hours of emotional torture, I could hear him snoring loudly when he eventually fell into a drink-infused sleep. I sat huddled in the dark. I don't know how long I was there, but eventually, my breathing slowed, and I felt an unusual calm and knowing sweep over me. It felt surreal yet so very real. My wise and beautiful soul told me, "Choose you, Jo, choose you." I instantly knew I was in a live-or-die situation, and to live, to be there for my children, I had to learn to love myself.

So, I did just that! I didn't falter; I stayed on course, and I did the work to change my life.

How you love yourself is how you teach others to love you.
—RUPI KAUR

That night in the dark, I sat with the realisation that I was a good person with a good heart, and no matter how many mistakes I had made, I certainly didn't deserve the life I was living. So, I made a pact with myself. I promised to learn to love myself and was 100% committed. I didn't know how, but I was determined. And it felt so right. I'm sure my Soul was cheering, dancing and singing.

The funny thing is, I had always been a little obsessed with Love, happiness and happy ever after, but had never taken the time to love myself, and instead, had felt inadequate, unworthy and not good enough for as long as I could remember. The way I allowed the voice in my head to speak to me was horrendous. (You know all about the voice; you have one, too, right? We all do. How does yours treat you?) According to me, I was fat, ugly, washed up, useless, pathetic, and just never got it right.

And without self-love, there is no self-esteem, no self-confidence, no self-honour and no self-respect. It's not a great foundation for living.

I would have outbursts and reactions, beg for Love, accept scraps of affection, play small, feel anxious and depressed, and put everyone else's needs above mine (not that I admitted I had needs). And all in all, it was exhausting, unfulfilling and soul-destroying. But I did it all with a smile, hiding my truth from the outside world. And I tried. I tried so hard to be successful, a good mum, for people to love me, to be seen, heard and understood, yet I never felt anything was enough, and I never got the results I so desperately wanted.

All I wanted was to be happy and feel loved. It sounds so simple, but I, like many, had to discover that it all starts with "Self."

Self-Love is the foundation for thriving and living your best life.

From Self-Love naturally comes self-respect, self-esteem, self-honour, self-care and self-confidence.

Suppose everyone in the world felt loved unconditionally and could find happiness and peace within. Imagine all those inner lights shining out. Wouldn't the world be a better place?

I went 30 years without much Love for myself, and the implications were huge because, after all, how we feel and think about ourselves affects our every thought, action and decision. Ending up in an abusive relationship was the end of a long road of self-destruction.

As a Self-Love Warrior Coach and Mentor, each day, I see clients in self-sabotage, self-loathing, repeating unhealthy cycles of behaviour, feeling stuck in life, and generally disliking themselves and disliking their life.

But when they decide to choose themselves, just as I did during that dark night on the sofa, they commit and do the work. It is beautiful and breathtaking, and magick really does happen. The trajectory of their life alters. Serendipitous things happen, passion is ignited, and they glow and vibrate at a higher frequency.

You need your own Love to save your heart.
—RITHVIK SINGH

Are you ready to glow, be empowered, Love and accept all of you, shine bright, and live in alignment with your Soul? Are you prepared to step into all of your glory and thrive?

I implore you to join me as a Pioneer of the Conscious Love Revolution. The world needs your light, and you, beautiful one, deserve to shine. You deserve all the Love you offer to everyone else. Yes, you deserve that same Love too.

I must warn you, though, Self-Love is not all fluffy. Yes, there is much gentleness, compassion, kindness, joy, honour and respect. There are affirmations, breathing, placing your hand on your beating heart, getting to know who you are, what you like, dislike, want and don't want, and rewiring a lot of previous programming.

But there is also a brutal side to Self-Love, which takes honesty, bravery, courage, determination, grit and fire. Because only when you can look at the darkest parts of yourself and choose to love them, only when you can accept your shame and love it, only when you can embrace your flaws and love them, only when you can feel all your emotions no matter how raw they are, and only when you can put your hand up if you misbehave, take responsibility and change your behaviour, this is when you have achieved Self-Love Mastery.

Quick Self-Love Tips:

1. Make friends with the voice in your head. It will always be there. Thank it, and treat it with Love, even if it is saying mean things. Then, start to reprogram it by replacing the mean stuff with nice, loving and pleasant language. "I am learning to love myself, and it feels good." "I am a nice person with a kind heart." "I am worthy, I am enough, I love you." Say as many nice things to yourself throughout the day. Go big. Be gushy!!!

2. Get to know yourself. Who are you? What do you like? How do you want to live your life? What lights up your Soul? What are your dreams and goals? What are your top five values? What brings you joy?

3. Write lists of your achievements and what you have experienced and overcome. I'm sure you have achieved, lived and survived. You are strong, brave, and resilient. You have the inner grit to learn to love yourself and shine your light!

HEAL THY SELF

Only when I accepted myself, approved of myself and truly loved myself did I make myself important and listen to my needs. Only then did I honour all of me, and the profound healing occurred.

Healing may be in an internal, solo job, but the effects can be felt far and wide. When you heal, find self-love and step into your worth, it is empowering, and you not only raise your vibration, but you help heal the world by creating a ripple effect of Love and healing to anyone or anything you encounter.

We heal the world by healing ourselves.

What is healing, and why does everyone need to heal?

Healing is honouring everything that has happened to you. Often, things happen in our life, and it is just our life. But it is important to understand that we are body, mind and Soul. Our life experiences are within us, in our cells, and if we don't honour what has happened, what we have experienced, then it gets stuck within us. It stays stagnant and is harmful.

I had a pregnancy termination when I was 14 years old. It tore me apart. I was a child playing at being an adult who craved Love and attention and looked for it in the wrong place. After going through the horrendous ordeal without much compassion from anyone in the hospital, I went home to get on with my life. Thirty years ago, no one offered counselling. So, I had a quiet weekend, returned to school, and we didn't talk about it again at home.

The emotional pain, shame and guilt I carried for the next 20 years was crippling at times. It resulted in depression and a deep ache in my womb.

Having four children didn't ease the pain, shame or guilt. And the two miscarriages I suffered later, I felt I deserved.

Only when I addressed my pain, shame and guilt around my abortion could the healing occur.

After several years of being on my healing journey, I attended a Coaching Conference. The coach presenting asked for a volunteer. Someone who had something that they wanted to let go of or to heal from. My Soul stirred, and I popped up my hand.

The coach used a regression technique on stage in front of hundreds of people, and I was transported to the hospital, where I saw my younger self going through an agonising experience. There I was, no more than a child, age 14, terrified, ashamed and in torment. It was a beautiful and special experience to give myself everything I needed during that time: kindness, compassion, reassurance and unconditional Love.

After taking her in my arms in a big squishy embrace, I said, "I love you; this is not your fault; you have made a mistake, and you are not bad. This does not define you. I love you endlessly and unconditionally, and I will always be here for you; you will be okay".

Our experiences and previous versions of ourselves are always within us: our 5, 10, 15 and 21-year-old. All of them are part of us. We must listen to their needs and give them what they needed during the times that perhaps those around us could not.

From that day, the deep pain in my womb cleared, and I have never felt the same heaviness around the experience again. Today, I use my past for good: I can connect with struggling teens because I still remember my teenage years of angst, trauma, and yuckiness.

Healing is a big deal and changes the trajectory of lives. It creates empowerment, confidence, and trust within yourself. It creates a choice to live on your terms with a healed and peaceful heart.

Healing is looking at unhealthy behaviours and actions and looking for the root cause, curiously looking at thoughts, beliefs and conditioning and deciding whether they are your truth and align with your Soul, and then forgiving or releasing, therefore not allowing the things that have happened to stop you from living and thriving.

When a healed person walks into a room, their aura is palpable, majestic and magnetic. Everyone wants to know their magick, but only some are prepared to step up and take the required journey.

Healing is understanding the difference between being a victim and victimhood behaviour. If you are or have been a victim, by admitting and claiming that you are or were a victim, owning it and, sitting with the pain and hurt and allowing it to flow through you, healing can begin.

A client who experienced sexual abuse during childhood was ready to address their past during a session. By naming it and discussing it, she stood tall and said, "I am a victim of sexual abuse, and it is not okay". Because she felt safe, she could look at the situation from the outside for the first time. Her hidden and pushed-down feelings and emotions surfaced: burning anger, hurt, and crushing pain, along with the disappointment of a stolen childhood and forgiveness of those who could not protect her every moment of each day.

Her healing had begun.

> *Healing takes courage, and we all have courage,*
> *even if we have to dig a little to find it.*
> —TORI AMOS

Healing is in the allowance of all emotions to flow through you, no matter how big. To not run and hide from them or to squash them down.

I used to put my feelings and emotions aside, thinking that others had it much worse than me, so who was I to be angry, hurt, and upset? This deflection caused the emotions to get stuck within, and eventually, my poor body, mind and Soul couldn't cope anymore: I suffered a nervous breakdown. We are human, and our emotions and feelings are to be honoured and not to be compared to others.

Healing is beautiful, painful, easy, raw, hard, dark, light, real, amazing, awful, and everything in between. It is worth the time and energy because healing sets you FREE!! Free from the shackles of your past. Free from the judgement of yourself and others. Free from emotional and physical pain. Free from self-sabotage.

Free from unhealthy coping mechanisms. Free from victimhood behaviour. Free from anything holding you back.

It's important to understand that healing is not linear; there are no hard and fast rules. It can be subtle, or it can be like a wrecking ball, and healing happens in layers. Starting at surface level and then going deeper.

To heal takes an enormous amount of self-discovery and honesty. Once you decide to hop on the healing train, there ain't no getting off. It's a forever journey. Why? Because hurt, pain, and trauma can continue to come your way, that is life, and the layers go deeper and deeper; healing is a cycle and a journey but one so very worth taking.

Healing is not all talking and feeling; it is moving energy, stagnant and stuck emotions, creating change, using dance, exercise, singing, yoga, breathing, ritual, chanting, and many other somatic experiences to move trauma, hurt, and pain. Healing can be painful at times, but it can be ecstatic, too.

So, the next time you are triggered, emotions will rise, and changes will occur physiologically, perhaps with tightness in your chest, a quickening of breath, jaw cleansing, or a pull in your stomach. You will want to react your usual way, maybe running away, shouting, panicking, withdrawing, acting up or becoming defensive. Stop and become aware of what is happening. Try to look on curiously; this is the sign that a wound has been touched. A wound that is asking to be healed.

Healing is a gift you give to yourself. Healing is powerful; it breaks chains and unhealthy behaviour patterns and creates freedom. When you heal yourself, you also heal lines of past, present and future generational trauma.

Help to heal the world, one person at a time, starting with you.

The human race doesn't need to suffer the way it does. Yes, some things happen in life, and life is full of polarity. Life and death, dark and light. There are natural disasters and atrocities, yet most suffering comes from within with regard to how we think and feel about ourselves and how we subsequently treat ourselves and respond to life.

Stop unnecessary suffering by choosing to love yourself and be your own best friend, cheerleader, and support crew. By appreciating the unique and magnificent gifts you bring to the world, you will heal your past and present and step into your magnetic glory.

Healing Mastery is looking at your life and saying, "Yes, this has happened. However, it will not define me, and I will not use it as an excuse to misbehave and continue unhealthy coping mechanisms because that will prevent me from succeeding and living life the way I want. I know I am responsible for how I respond to life, and I choose to heal, get better and live fully."

Raise the vibration and frequency of the earth by living from an operating platform of Conscious Love.

I invite you to join me as a Pioneer of the Conscious Love Revolution.

Healing Tips:

1. Practice the 3 A's of **Awareness**, **Acknowledgement**, **Acceptance**. Become aware of the need to heal, acknowledge and accept it. (Without the 3 A's, you're in denial).

2. When you are triggered, rather than respond, remove yourself gracefully from the situation and address the wound. Be kind, compassionate and honest with yourself.

3. Honour any emotions using the 3 A's. Be aware of the emotion, acknowledge it by naming it, i.e., I am feeling sad, and then accept it. Then, place your hand on your heart, allow yourself

to feel, and sit with the emotion. If necessary, set a timer for a few minutes, so you know you are safe.

CONSCIOUS LOVE

You cannot escape pain and hurt, no matter how fast you run or how well you hide. They are an inevitable part of life. You can try all you might to protect your heart from heartbreak. Or you can choose to live from Conscious Love, and love yourself wholeheartedly, heal your past, present and future and step into Love with pure and true vulnerability. With a heart so fully open, it blooms beautifully and shines bright.

Conscious Love is how we give and receive Love, position ourselves in the world and choose to live.

> *What happens when people open their hearts?*
> *They get better.*
> —HARUKI MURAKAM

At 38 years old, I finally loved myself after finding Self-Love in the most unusual circumstances after the man who vowed to love me abused me more than I had abused myself. Today, I am at peace with what happened, grateful even. It was a tiring struggle because I had been doing a great job of keeping myself down and emotionally beating myself up, but his actions helped me hit rock bottom.

It's wild how we humans usually have to hit rock bottom to make changes to our lives. However, mediocrity is dangerous territory too. Because every day, I hear people complaining about their lives being far from their dream life, yet not too bad to be bothered making any long-term changes. How many relationships do you see where one or both seem miserable yet stay together or don't make conscious efforts to change? And how many people do you know who work in a job that drains the living daylights out of them, yet they don't search for another option?

Once I found Self-Love and did a lot of healing, I realised I had been living my entire life from a platform of FEAR. Fear had been my filter, not Love.

Whenever I meet a new client, I feel their Fear, as they lack self-worth and self-love and look outside for the answers that are always within. *Recently an 18-year-old client who completed a 6-week intensive course and jumped into self-love and living from Love wrote to thank me because she is rocking life, taking chances, trying new things, meeting new people, and genuinely enjoying her life.*

Magick really does happen, and rapid changes are there for the taking.

The Fear filter holds us back, stops us from stepping into our worth, truth and power, keeps us locked in mediocrity, allows us to play small, and keeps us stuck.

> *Fear is where there is no love.*
> *Love is where there is no fear.*
> —AXL ROSE

From Fear to my detriment, I had clung on to things and people for way too long, tried too hard, given all of myself away, never set boundaries, didn't think I was important, had a chronic addiction to people pleasing and spent so much time trying to find my worth by being the busiest person I could be; as a mum of four, running businesses, doing everything at home, joining the PTA, doing charity work and much more. Nothing worked. It was draining; I was bone-achingly exhausted, and my Soul was watching on in confusion and wondering why I wasn't listening when she spoke to me and asked for something different.

Our Soul chooses Love each time because Love is always the answer. Loving thoughts. Loving behaviour. Loving actions.

So, when our humanness, programming and conditioning take over, we often operate from Fear by making decisions, reacting, and having thoughts and feelings from Fear such as discomfort, disgruntled, discontent, unhappiness, depression, anger, sad, unfulfilled, bitterness, resentful, hopelessness, helpless, worthless... take your pick!

We feel misaligned because what we are doing differs from what our Soul chooses.

Our Souls signed up for this human experience to grow, learn and evolve. Isn't it time to let your Soul sparkle, shine and have a flippin' good time?

Unsurprisingly, there is so much Fear in the world. We are programmed to live from Fear. Just look around. The news broadcasts stories of recession, war, murder, corruption, illness, etc. TV shows demonstrate life needs to be full of drama to make it interesting. Fashion magazines show us we must look a certain way to be attractive. Social media shares a glorified image of life, and all install Fear. Fear strangles dreams, cuts off creativity, and is a foundation of instability.

I look back at my past and wonder whether any of it was true Love. Of course, I loved people: my partner, children, family and friends. But is Love based on Fear actually love at all?

Love is at the opposite end of the spectrum as Fear. Both are equally potent.

If Love is pure, expansive, and of high frequency, then why had much of the Love I felt in my past created angst, worry, insecurity, pain, neediness and stress, all low-frequency emotions? Was it ever Love?

Love based on Fear is a poor version of Love and all that Love has to offer because Love is uplifting and feels good.

Like most of my clients, as I became more enlightened and aligned with my Soul, it became apparent that operating from Fear wasn't working for me (psst, it doesn't work for anyone!). It felt off, icky and dense, and I didn't like the feeling of heavy energy and low-frequency emotions, so the only other answer is and will always be Love.

As the creator of my life, I take responsibility for it. As a spiritual and energetic being, I know what I give out, I get back, everything from the thoughts in my head to my behaviour, morals, values and the energy I give out to the world. The Law of Attraction is one I believe in greatly; therefore, living at high frequency is important to me.

Living in higher frequency emotions and consciously choosing Love feels wonderful, spacious, and free. Love is always the answer.

You are so powerful, my dear one. I want you to hear this message; it is for you. You are unique, amazing, wonderful and magnificent. The world needs your light. Remember, every one light fills a room of darkness. You have everything within you to live the life of your dreams in alignment with your Soul, a life that inspires and energises and feels good and uplifting. You are not here to suffer and only survive. It's time to thrive and lead the world in a different direction towards the light.

> *To fear Love is to fear life, and those who fear life are*
> *already three points dead.*
> —BERTRAND RUSSELL

Conscious Love is without blame, judgement, or allowing ego to take over and is with kindness, compassion, care and peace.

I took the time to find Self-Love, heal, and step into my truth. None of it was an accident. And choosing to live consciously from Love aligns with my Soul, makes me the best version of myself, and helps me pass on my message, experience, expertise and knowledge to help others heal.

So, together, we can stand strong to help heal and change the world with light.

Loving consciously, people, the planet, animals, and yourself all takes practice. Using enquiring questions and being curious helps. Ask yourself questions such as:

Is this a loving thought?

Am I being judgemental?

How can I turn my judgment to compassion?

Is this belief or opinion my truth, do I truly believe it, and why do I?

Am I following or leading?

Is my behaviour how I want it to be?

Am I listening and understanding what is being said?

Am I acting from unconditional Love, or does my Love have conditions?

In meditation, I have had visions of eutopia, light and beauty in this world—a world without drama, hatred, envy, insecurities, or rage. Instead, there is a bright world full of pure white light where people enjoy relationships and friendships and then move on because the part of their journey together ended. They go their separate ways without the need for revenge, bitterness or anger—a world where everyone is full of self-love and takes responsibility for their healing and life.

Tips for living from Conscious Love:

1. View the world as a giant playground and see everything in it as an opportunity for your Soul to learn, grow and evolve.

2. Use Clear, Concise and Calm communication. Speak to people as you love them. Check your energy before communicating; you can't hide energy (for example, if you're angry, work on that before entering into communication). Use a loving and pleasant tone. Be assertive, not passive, aggressive or passive-aggressive.

3. Do things that light you up, bring you joy and enhance a peaceful heart. The more you can do to raise your vibration and keep yourself healthy and happy, the more you can offer the world and others.

My Soul's purpose is to inject more Love into the world by giving and receiving Love with an open, vulnerable heart to everyone I encounter and to guide others on their self-love and healing journey. Each day I choose Love, and you can too. I am Love, you are Love, and Love is powerful. Is my life perfect? Ha, don't be silly; perfection doesn't exist. But it is great because I have learned to operate from Love even in a crisis or adversity. And my wish is that you do too.

Self-Love, Healing and choosing Conscious Love have changed my life. Every day, I wake up excited for the day. I am a confident momma who can hold all her children through their ups and downs in life. I approach drastic situations with a clear head and an open heart. I know I can and may get hurt along the way, but there is no Fear, only openness to learn, grow and evolve for the good of humanity.

No more crappy relationships, giving and putting myself last, settling, mediocrity, playing small, doing things because I should, no more feeling awful and exhausted, put-downs, and no more going to bed and wondering when life will get better. Because life is better, life is what I attract.

What is your Soul calling you to do, and how do you want to live your life?

My mission is for every individual to feel beautiful, empowered and worthy of Love.

Why? Because if every individual sees and feels their worth, stands in the power of self-love, loves themselves and others unconditionally, heals, seeks joy, rejects Fear and embraces Conscious Love, the world will shine like a beacon.

As a Self-Love Warrior, Quantum Coach & Mentor, my superpower is embodying Self-Love and showing others how to do it too. I help clients embody who they truly are and see their infinite beauty, worth and power to thrive, kick-ass and live confidently and fully.

Please join me as a Pioneer of the Conscious Love Revolution in my "Loving Warrior Goddess Soul Circle" Facebook group, or you can find me on Instagram at **the_happinesshustler**.

You are worthy, enough, important, loveable, exquisite, unique and magical. It's time to shine and lead with light.

Much Love, light, peace and sparkles.

Jo (aka The Happiness Hustler)

Please join me as a Pioneer of the Conscious Love Revolution in my 'Loving Warrior Goddess Soul Circle' Facebook group - https://www.facebook.com/groups/warriorgoddesssoulcircle , or you can find me on Instagram at **the_happinesshustler** or Joanne Webb on Facebook.

Alexis Quiterio

As a former competitive athlete of 16 years, Alexis believes we can be, do, and have it all. Here to empower your growth in this next chapter of life, she has a deep passion for wellness, healthy habits, and living fully. Get ready to embrace the energy and experience she's infused in these pages as she supports your journey of becoming your best self.

Discover Your Power Within

by Alexis Quiterio

PREFACE

> *"The question that faces the strategic decision maker is not what he should do tomorrow. It is, what do we have to do today to be ready for an uncertain tomorrow?"*
>
> —PETER DRUCKER

When I was younger, my parents told me I could be, do, and have anything my heart desires. But there was a catch… I would have to work hard, really hard. At the time I just thought of getting good grades and trying my hardest as it pertained to a job. Little did I know about the mental and physical component as well.

"If I'm willing to put in the work, my life will be everything I want and more. Easy." I thought.

As I got older and took on more responsibilities, I kept hearing narratives from adults that differed from that in which my parents taught me. Those outside voices indicated I couldn't have it all, that everything was a give and a take, a this **or** that.

"You can't have your cake and eat it too."

"You can't have the sun and the rain at the same time."

"You can't have the best of both worlds."

But as I worked on developing my own reality and beliefs, I came to find those people were only focusing on one piece of the pie, whereas I was focusing on all 3; strategic decisions, healthy habits, and personal development. Why couldn't I have it all? Isn't that what life is about? Becoming, experiencing, and having everything I've ever desired?

I wanted that fairytale love with a partner **and** to love myself unconditionally. I wanted to travel for work, have a 4-hour workday, **and** be financially free. I wanted to spend time with my friends and family **and** have time to pursue my passions. I wanted to maintain a good physique **and** excel in my career.

I believed I could be, do, and have it all. So, that's what I set out to do. This is my story of how I went for it, and so can you.

BE THE 2%

Don't be fooled, nothing worth having comes easy, otherwise everyone would have it. Studies show 98% of people die without fulfilling their goals and dreams. As my mentor always told me, the graveyard is the richest place in the world.

It doesn't matter where you are in life or how old you are, you can become the 2% that achieve "success." The best time to decide was a second ago and the best time to start is **now**.

YOUR REFLECTION IS YOUR FUEL

I want you to take a moment and reflect on something significant. Think back to where you were five years ago. Remember what you were doing, who you loved, and what you wanted in life? How did you feel? Were you happy or feeling lost?

Now, close your eyes and let those memories sink in.

Next, shift your focus to the present moment. Think about where you are now, what you're doing, who you love, and what you want in life. Are you happy? Do you have a clear sense of direction?

Take a minute to process these thoughts.

As you reflect, you'll likely notice a mix of emotions. Some reflections may bring a smile to your face, while others might evoke a sense of longing or frustration because you're not where you want to be... yet. However, when you look at the big picture, chances are you have achieved at least some of what you once wished for.

Acknowledge the progress you've made and celebrate the steps you've taken towards your goals. If you find yourself longing for more, use this reflection as fuel to practice the roadmap I lay out for you in the following pages so you can change your future based on your decision to commit.

If you're satisfied with your reflection that's something to be proud of. This is an opportunity for more growth so you can reach that next level and *discover your power within.*

DON'T STAY BLIND

Today, we face a common challenge of being bombarded with options, distractions, and constant stimulation. There's always a new TV show to watch, a social media feed to scroll through, notifications to answer, and products to buy. If we're not careful, the next few decades will pass us by in the blink of an eye, leaving us regretting the things we never did, the places we never visited, and the person we never became.

Living a distracted, unintentional, and unhappy life will lead to missed opportunities down the road. That's not the life you want to live, is it?

This doesn't have to be your reality. It won't be. Here's how.

A QUARTER LIFE CRISIS AND A DECISION

My wakeup call came shortly after I finished college. I was three weeks into my corporate job when I was asked to alter my work ethic. My boss asked me to slow down on task completion because I was getting things done faster than our product could be produced.

In that moment, a sliver of my truth emerged—I'm not working to get paid; I'm working to make a difference. Naturally, I became curious as to what that looked like outside of this job. What were some of my other interests? Likes and dislikes? Strengths and weaknesses? Potential of the mindset and habits I had developed through competitive sports?

I needed answers. So, I went on a journey to discover them.

I returned home that afternoon and started searching for answers. I grabbed my phone and opened social media in hopes of distracting myself. I didn't know what to do or where to start. No one teaches you about this stuff and up to this point, I hadn't heard this situation from anyone else. I felt alone.

As I scrolled through social media, I came across a girl I competed against in high school gymnastics. We knew of each other through the sport, but never officially met or interacted. I started following her on social media in college as she publicly shared her fitness journey.

At the time, I didn't have the self-awareness to understand why I felt envy towards her, but at a minimum I understood she was doing something I wish I had the courage to do, which was share my journey. I always felt a calling to lead people and felt as though the lessons, characteristics, and experience my 17 years of competitive sports taught me was valuable and could inspire others. But no, instead I was undergoing a quarter life crisis and staring at her latest post.

Her post was referencing a podcast that positively impacted her. Even though I wasn't used to reading books or self-educating outside of the traditional school system, curiosity led me to listen. I opened the Podcast app on my phone.

I listened to this personal development podcast and learned how our thoughts influence our actions and our actions impact our results. I decided to dive deeper down this path, acknowledging that my current thoughts and actions weren't getting me where I wanted to be.

7.5 years later, I'm still grateful for that post. Because of her, I made a single decision that changed my life forever.

35,000 OPPORTUNITIES

Would you agree that your life is the sum of all the decisions you've made up to this point?

Would you agree if you hung out with five millionaires you would be the sixth?

Would you agree if you exercised 3-5x per week and ate healthy that you could have a 6-pack?

Would you agree if you showed up to a networking event and made an effort to interact with others that you could leave with new friends?

Would you agree if you asked for something you want your chances of receiving it would increase because you showed interest?

Would you agree if you explored your curiosities and took intentional action, as I did with that podcast, your life can change for the better?

Research shows we make 35,000 conscious decisions on a daily basis. Meaning, we have tens of thousands of opportunities to change and enhance our lives every single day! Imagine making the decision to call a friend that's been on your mind. They share how you made their day and invite you to an event that night. You attend and end up meeting the love of your life. Or consider the choice to adopt a healthy lifestyle after your doctor's warning, leading to shedding 70 pounds, feeling full of energy, mentally sharper, and overall happier and healthier within just six months. Every minute, there's a chance to transform our lives for the better through the decisions we make.

You might be wondering, "With so many decisions to make each day, how do I know which ones are best for me?" That's a great question! The cool thing is, we have full control over the decisions we make and the actions we take. We can achieve our dreams and desires in life, but it requires dedication beyond what we might have expected. So, take a step and change just one decision today. It can be the start of a new chapter or the beginning of something incredible. The choice is yours.

HEALTHY HABITS

> *"Healthy habits are learned in the same way as unhealthy ones—through practice."*
> —WAYNE DYER

Just like plugging in your phone when it's about to die or watering your plants regularly for them to grow, certain habits have a cause-and-effect relationship. Healthy habits that lead to reaching your goals are no different. The key lies in the small, intentional actions you take daily, which can make all the difference in achieving happiness and success. It's the simple choices that create the biggest impact.

IDENTIFY, DON'T JUSTIFY

There are two reasons why people lack healthy habits.

1. They lack the knowledge of *how* to be healthy.
2. They don't care.

Have you ever chosen a Caesar salad over a cheeseburger thinking it was the healthier option, only to find out that the Caesar dressing makes it less healthy than the cheeseburger? If this is new information to you, you're not alone! It just shows there's room to learn.

On the other hand, if you knew this fact about the dressing but failed to order it on the side, it demonstrates your lack of care.

Our brains are smart; they develop habits to make our daily actions easier and more automatic. These habits support our energy and the life we want, acting as little power-ups that recharge our body and mind, helping us perform at our best every day. They're nourishment that support our strength and growth. They're a shield that keep us safe, healthy, and happy on our life's journey.

By embracing healthy habits that align with your future goals, you can be, do, and have it all. It's like cause and effect—take intentional action and live the life you desire.

If you want more happiness and success in your life, start by recognizing where you currently stand. You can only make improvements when you identify what needs to change.

In the upcoming sections, I'll share three habits that will transform your life. You'll gain mental clarity, improve your appearance, and develop the traits to achieve all your dreams and more.

HABIT 1: REFLECTIVE JOURNALING

*"Everything is in a big magnifying glass and you look at
everything in detail. You only have room to see what you
want to see."*
—SUSAN SAANDHOLLAND

Ever had someone tell you to "talk it out" when you're feeling emotional? It can feel liberating to express yourself and understand your true feelings. Similarly, when someone advises you to "write it down," you might be surprised how it helps you make sense of your thoughts, emotions, and what to do next. It's your secret weapon.

Psychology shows that writing things down offers countless benefits. It clears your mind, helps you understand emotions, make decisions, manage stress, and take action. It's a powerful tool for your well-being.

If you're anything like me, when I used to hear the word "journaling" I couldn't help but think back to my "Dear Diary" days in grade school where I confessed my love for crushes and wrote secret thoughts I couldn't share with anyone. As I got older, I abandoned the practice, only to pick it back up years later.

Today, journaling is an essential practice and what I consider to be a competitive advantage. The more time I take to reflect and understand how I feel and why, the more problems I solve, self-love I experience, and aligned future I build.

Let's set aside any preconceived notions and embrace the journey of self-discovery through journaling. Don't dismiss it as silly; it holds boundless potential. Trust me, it transformed my life, and it can do the same for you.

THE JAR OF JOY

My relationship with journaling was rekindled one New Year's Eve in my early 20's. I stumbled on a profound idea: a gratitude jar. With a transparent jar, sticky notes, and a pen, I began to document moments of gratitude and cherished memories throughout my day. During the year, my jar grew with memories from laughter-filled nights with friends to simple acts of kindness. It overflowed with happiness and joy. I started calling it my "Jar of Joy."

One year later, as I dumped out the jar to read the notes aloud, I found myself in a sea of gratitude and growth, feeling more present and evolved throughout my days than I ever had.

That initial decision one year ago, turned into my biggest gift; a practice that evolved into capturing lessons and personal growth through journaling. From a simple jar of sticky notes to a hand-held journal, it became a powerful practice I continue to this day, one that shapes my perspective, brings me clarity, and illuminates the beauty in everyday moments.

Today, nine years later, the power of journaling publicized itself in the form of a book, to share my personal experiences with you, hoping you will one day do the same.

A COMPASS TO GUIDE YOU

As my documentation practice evolved, I stumbled upon a form of journaling that goes beyond the traditional methods. I call it "Reflective Journaling," and guess what? It's super easy to start. Are you ready?

At the end of each day, simply jot down what happened. Capture moments that made you smile, laugh, happy, sad, or frustrated. Let it all flow onto the pages. That's it. You're documenting your day.

Now, you might be wondering, "What's so special about that?" Let me tell you … everything! Without even realizing it, you'll witness the magic of this practice as it transforms your day-to-day life. You'll record events, insights, thoughts, feelings, and even those small victories. Before you know it, these reflections become the lessons that make up the roadmap of your life's journey.

The best part? You only need 10-20 minutes each day! That's way less time than mindlessly scrolling through social media. Be intentional with your time. Set an alarm 20 minutes before bedtime and unwind your thoughts without any judgment or structure. You'll be amazed how much clarity and growth this simple practice creates.

Imagine adopting this practice as if you were wiping dust off a mirror. At first, the mirror might show a blurry image, making reality hard to see. But as you diligently clean and polish the mirror, the reflection becomes clearer and more accurate. Similarly, when you reflect and write consistently, you wipe away the mental dust, allowing yourself to see your thoughts and feelings more distinctly and understand who you truly are.

I've experienced the power of this practice firsthand. It became, and continues to be, an invaluable tool to conquer overthinking, understand fear, and gain emotional control. Reflective Journaling turned me into my own therapist, fueling personal growth and self-discovery. When we clearly acknowledge the actions we want to repeat and those we want to leave behind, we take back control of our lives.

So, whether you seek transformation, emotional healing, or a compass to guide you, embrace the transformative power of Reflective Journaling. Let your words be a portal into your deepest thoughts and experiences. Allow your reflections to reveal patterns that serve you and those that don't. Let your decisions guide you back on the path towards a life where you can truly be yourself, purposefully do what you love, and joyfully have it all.

HABIT 2: EXERCISE

> *"There are no shortcuts in life because you can't find a*
> *shortcut on a path you've never walked."*
> —KYLE A. HERRON

Before we jump in, I want to share something important: achieving a healthy body and mind is 85% about what you eat and 15% about exercise. Amidst modern technology, the majority of people are easily distracted and remain sedentary, leading to reduced movement. Below, I'll share my proven and reliable practices to help infuse more exercise into your day. These small changes can lead to massive transformations. Let's get into it!

AFTER RETIREMENT

For 15 years, gymnastics was my life. From the tender age of 3, I dedicated myself to the sport, pouring my heart and soul into every practice and every competition. In college, I competed in pole-vaulting at the Division 1 level, demonstrating the same commitment to excellence as before. But when the time came to step away from the world of athletics, I found myself facing a new reality.

Shortly after I stopped working out, I realized the detrimental effects of a sedentary lifestyle on my mental and physical well-being. I sought to reintegrate exercise into my post-sport life as I experienced mental fog, physical fatigue, and mood swings. I wasn't my usual self. All I had was a desire to be better and the curiosity to explore what this new form of exercise looked like for me.

I experimented with various activities, ultimately embracing weightlifting, acro yoga, hiking, and playful movement as sustainable and enjoyable options. These exercises became my anchor, providing clarity, stress relief, and a renewed sense of balance, hope, and joy in my life.

My goal is to provide you with easy-to-start or easy-to-continue strategies and insights to stick with a healthy lifestyle for years to come. It will take effort and intention, but like anything else, once you gain momentum, it gets easier and more enjoyable.

YOUR BODY IS A STATUS SYMBOL

Over the course of 8 years, I lived in 5 different cities, but I never let that stop me from taking care of my body, nurturing my mind, and excelling in my career. How did I do it? Simple—I remained committed to feeling good, looking good, and staying healthy, no matter how busy life got.

Imagine a life where you genuinely liked the person looking back at you in the mirror every day. How would you act? How would you dress? How would you show up in the world? My guess is that you'd feel happier, full of energy, confident, and achieve more success.

Regular physical exercise is not just about how you look; it's a mental and physical test of your daily challenges. Each repetition becomes a commitment to push through hardships. Every workout completed signifies progress, growth, and improvement. Every time you show up to exercise, especially when you think you don't have time, you build confidence that you can do anything you set your mind to.

Having a strong physique commands respect before you even speak. It's like a status symbol, showing your commitment to yourself and your potential. You only need 20 minutes per day and I bet you can find that time easily… cue mindlessly scrolling social media or binge-watching TV, which is robbing you of your potential, happiness, and success.

It's time to say goodbye to old habits and step into the person you know you're meant to be. Say this affirmation out loud:

"I, (your name), promise to dedicate at least 20 minutes to movement every day. Life may throw challenges, but I'm determined to better my body, mind, and life, and I promise to show up no matter what."

THE WHAT

It's time to discover activities that bring you joy and excitement. Whether it's dancing, running, hiking, biking, or practicing yoga, choose movement that's fun! When you enjoy what you do, sticking to it becomes easier, and exercise becomes a regular part of your life.

If you don't have the time or mental space to figure it out on your own, that's okay and very common. This is why many people hire a trainer, so they can focus on showing up while the trainer takes care of the planning. I'll share more resources at the end of this chapter to support you in this journey!

THE HOW

Before we get all excited to start something new, I'm going to remind you, be realistic and keep it simple. It's not the time to get all fancy with your exercise and overcommit. For instance, if you don't currently exercise and think you're going to start working out 5x per week for 2 hours per day, disappointment is soon to befallen you. Keep it simple and go from 0-2 days per week for 20 minutes. In one month, increase that to 3x per week for 20 minutes. Take small steps and gradually build up to maintain this new habit.

TIMING MATTERS

Every evening, prepare for your workout by laying out your clothes or packing your gym bag before bed. This simple act reduces decision fatigue in the morning and increases the likelihood of sticking to your workout.

The goal is to make it easy and doable.

This is what I've found to work best for me in different phases of life. Life will get busy, but by exercising in the morning, you free up more time to enjoy the rest of your day and have lasting energy for everything you want to do!

CONFUSE PEOPLE

One simple thing can boost mental clarity, decrease anxiety, and help you lose weight. It's a magic four-letter word that most of us can do: walk.

Got lots of emails to answer? Take a walk. Feeling overwhelmed? Talk it out with yourself while walking. Need to process thoughts? Walk it out. Have a short break at work? Go for a walk. Ate too much? Walking aids in digestion. Sore from exercising? Walk to promote low-impact muscle recovery. Need to make a big decision? Think it through while walking.

Research shows that walking has amazing benefits. It gets your blood flowing, nourishing your brain with nutrients and oxygen. This boosts your mood, creativity, and overall health. It might not seem like much, but profound results are found in small actions done on a consistent basis.

Walking while working has become my favorite "life hack." Whether outside or on a stationary desk treadmill, your boss will notice your improved productivity, and your loved ones will wonder why you're so happy. Remember, you continuously do what *feels good*!

HABIT 3: MORNING ROUTINE

Research shows the first 20 minutes after we wake up is called the "alpha stage," proven to be the "gateway to the subconscious mind." It is in these first 20 minutes of waking up that our subconscious mind is most impressionable, soaking up the information we feed it like a sponge.

Knowing that, wouldn't you agree waking up and looking at the news or using social media is not the best way to start your day if you want to be, do, and have everything you've ever dreamed? I would, and do, avoid it like the plague.

CURIOUS ABOUT PEACE

In the bustling city of New York, lived a young woman named Lily. Her mornings were a chaotic frenzy, always chasing time and barely making it to work on time. One spring morning, as she shut her balcony door before leaving for work, she noticed a middle-aged woman out on her balcony across the way. Because the buildings were so close, Lily could see how serene and radiant the woman was, reading her book, writing on a notepad, and taking deep breaths as she lifted her head to the sky, smiling. Lily was intrigued but shut the door and raced to catch the subway.

For the next several weeks, Lily saw the middle-aged woman out on her balcony doing the same thing. She found herself envious of her neighbors' peace as she found herself always rushing. With curiosity piqued, Lily decided to say something.

Once Lily introduced herself to the woman, Mrs. Emerald, she learned of the secret to Mrs. Emerald's harmonious start to the day: a morning routine.

Mrs. Emerald helped Lily understand the power of a morning routine, comparing it to tuning an instrument before a symphony, emphasizing the importance of aligning our minds, bodies, and spirits each morning. It was critical, she shared, to set the tone for her day.

Mrs. Emerald shared how her morning routine transformed her life, cultivating stillness amidst chaos, and connecting with her inner self. This ritual empowered her to be present, focused, and productive throughout the day, enhancing her overall well-being, especially in a bustling city like New York.

Inspired, Lily realized that her mornings lacked purpose and self-care. She yearned to start her day intentionally. With newfound understanding, she started by setting her alarm earlier and experimented with a routine that included gentle stretches, gratitude, and a nourishing breakfast.

As Lily embraced her morning routine, the frantic pace faded, replaced by a tranquil rhythm. She felt centered, focused, and open-hearted. Her mind grew clearer, and her energy became more directed. Her morning routine became the foundation for her day. It guided her towards a life filled with purpose and intention. She became the conductor, directing her own symphony.

FEELINGS DON'T LIE

Imagine waking up to a morning routine that sets a positive tone for the day, awakening your mind and nourishing your soul. Many go through life without considering how their actions impact them.

So, ask yourself, how do you feel in the mornings? Are you stressed, anxious, and tired? Or do you wake up feeling energized, focused, and optimistic?

Do you reach for your phone first thing in the morning and scroll through social media like it's the morning newspaper? Or do you start the day without your phone as you go through a mediation, intention, and reflection practice?

Are you on autopilot as you get ready for the day, unaware of how it feels to pick outfit, brush your teeth, or eat breakfast? Or are you in the moment, getting ready for your day one step at a time, sipping your coffee in between and thinking of the opportunities that lay ahead?

Be honest with yourself and think about the reality your current morning actions create. Turn to your Reflective Journaling practice to identify the actions that bring you negativity and angst versus peace and ease. If you want calm, clarity, and peace at the start of your day, it's time to consider creating a morning routine.

LIFE'S BEST KEPT SECRET

You might be thinking, "I don't have time for a morning routine," or "I don't need one," or "I don't know where to start."

Well, here's the beauty of morning routines: you can make them your own! It's all about strategic decisions. You get to choose what you want to include and how long you want it to be. Let's explore what creating a morning routine that aligns with what you want to achieve could look like.

Sam is aiming for a promotion at work, and he's determined to make it happen with a morning routine that supports his goals. Here's what he does:

- He sets his alarm 20 minutes early to read 10 pages of a managerial book, preparing his mind for the new role he envisions.

- Sam practices gratitude, visualizing himself already in the promoted position.

- He does some stretching exercises to get his blood flowing, which helps him think clearly and remain patient throughout the day.

- Sam leaves the house a few minutes early, showing his commitment to his work by arriving on time.

Hailey wants to start her day with less anxiety, but she's not sure where it's coming from. Here are some morning routine ideas to support her:

- First thing in the morning, Hailey avoids opening any social media apps or using her phone for the first two hours to create a calm start to her day.

- She writes down three things she's grateful for, setting a positive tone for the day and making it easier to notice other small things to be grateful for.

- Hailey takes 15 slow, deep breaths to find a moment of stillness and peace.

- She spends 20 minutes on exercise to get her blood flowing, focusing on the mind-to-muscle connection to feel the exercise working.

- Lastly, Hailey reads five pages of a personal development book to better understand her emotions and learn practices to support her growth.

When you adopt a morning routine, you're creating the life you desire by acting "as if" you're already where you want to be. It sets the tone for the day, signaling to your subconscious who you want to become.

If you want to see change, start by examining your daily habits and how they influence your decisions. It might feel strange and time-consuming at first, but with practice, it becomes a new, empowering habit that opens doors for growth and opportunity.

Let each sunrise guide you to embrace the power of a morning routine.

DON'T WAIT, INTEGRATE

Don't leave your dream life where you can be, do, and have it all up to chance. Learning and intention is nothing without action. Thinking and hoping doesn't get you results. If you want to make a change, new types of action are required. That includes taking immediate action before motivation fades.

Have you ever wondered what you're capable of? What your potential is if you actually showed up in peak mental and physical shape every day? The hardest action to take is 0-1, but this initial motivation and hope you received from reading these pages is like the wind behind your sails; use this excitement and curiosity to take your first action as quickly as possible!

Can I be honest with you? That's why you're here, years later, wishing you started back then, looking back and wondering what your life would look like today if you took immediate action last time. It's time to wake up and stop wishing, hoping, and praying. Start **ACTING.**

Try this…

If you're finishing this chapter in the morning, try to incorporate "walking while working" into your day as you answer emails or phone calls. Exercise is underway!

If you're reading this at night, grab a notepad or open the Notes app on your phone and start to write about your day. Reflective Journaling is underway!

It's not about being perfect… it's about starting today and making small decisions with intentional actions that align with who you're meant to be.

Look, we all make mistakes; we're human. But don't be like most people and make the same mistakes over and over again expecting a different result. Albert Einstein calls that insanity. Let today be the start of your story. Let today be the day you'll look back on and say, "I am the happiest, strongest, and wealthiest I've ever been because I made one decision to take action and do something different."

I BELIEVE IN YOU

I'll be honest with you, unlocking your potential won't happen alone. It requires community, coaches, and commitment, just like it did for me. Use the resources I've provided below. Surround yourself with people who are smarter than you in the areas you want to improve, those who have achieved the results you seek. Connect with me and like-minded individuals on social media to support each other on this journey. Make a promise to yourself that you'll be relentless in your pursuit.

My goal is to help you discover the warrior within you, your infinite potential. To remind you that you're alive today so you can learn, grow, and experience the beauty of life. I want to hear from you 1, 3, 5 years from now about how your life changed because you started today. Stop me in person, reach out to me on social media, and share with our community!

Life is waiting for you to be, do, and have it all. If you're willing to put in the work, you'll discover your power within and experience the depth of happiness and love that's waiting for you. You can do it. GO!

For those eager to connect with Alexis, explore collaboration opportunities, or seek her guidance, visit her website alexisquiterio.com and click on "Discover Your Power Within." For immediate connection, follow her on social media @alexisquiterio and subscribe to her newsletter to stay up to date with events, insights, and tools to support your journey of self-discovery and growth.

https://stan.store/alexisquiterio

We Help *YOU* Become a Center of Influence!

CENTER OF INFLUENCE COMMUNITY

Coaches, Consultants, Speakers, and Thought Leaders
Join a Community that Fully Supports You!

*What Would Becoming a Best-Selling
Author do for Your Business?*

Find out by being in one of our unique anthologies!

www.centerofinfluencecommunity.com

www.ingramcontent.com/pod-product-compliance
Lightning Source LLC
Chambersburg PA
CBHW071329120626
46546CB00002B/495